LET'S WRITE A PICTURE BOOK

A Practical Guide

Every Great Journey Starts by Taking the First Step!

Matt B Lewis

Let's Write A Picture Book, A Practical Guide

Copyright © 2021 Matt B Lewis

All rights reserved. No part of this publication may be reproduced, stored in a retrieval system, or transmitted in any form or by any means electronic, mechanical, photocopying, recording, or otherwise without the prior written permission of the publisher and copyright owner.

Published by Gecko Tales Publishing

ISBN-13: 978-0-992393-49-6

A catalogue record for this work is available from the National Library of Australia

TABLE OF CONTENTS

Introduction	4
What Is A Picture Book?	6
Before We Start	9
Idea Creation	11
Character Creation	18
The Plot	26
The Problem	29
Build Your World	33
The 3 Acts	37
Tell A Good Story	43
Time To Write	58
Your First Draft	67
Steps To Editing	75
Manuscript Assessment	80
The Illustrations	83
Print Jargon	91
The Manuscript	98
Thumbnailing	105
The Storyboard	108
Character Creation 2.0	111
Using Reference	115
Composition	120
Cover Art	124
Portfolio Perfection	129
Document Setup	133
Path To Publication	142
Self-Publish	159
Literary Agents	168
Where To From Here?	178

INTRODUCTION

WELCOME to the world of **KIDSLIT!**
So who's this guy, and why has he written this book?

My name is **MATT B LEWIS**, and it was only 4 short years ago that I was sitting where you are today. I knew I wanted to write a story for my kids, but I didn't have the first clue about how to go about it or even where to start. Does this sound familiar?

Over the last few years, I have written and/or illustrated over 20 books.

What's my **BIG PROMISE?**

By the time you work through this book, you are going to have everything you need to create a picture book children will love, that you are super proud of and that you can either submit to a publisher or self-publish.

Now, many people stop at the idea of writing a children's picture book, they may have a great idea, but then self-doubt sneaks in, they think to themselves, 'I have never written a book before, I have no experience!' That is perfectly normal and it's OK, I have you covered. I designed this book for the absolute novice, with simple, easy to follow chapters and exercises.

So, WHY buy this book when there are literally hundreds of other books on writing children's picture books? The simple answer is, I have been where you are!

Once upon a time (pun intended) I was a novice children's book author too. Confronted with overwhelming technical information and nothing on the actual art of crafting a picture book, I was **LOST**.

That's where this book is different. With minimal technical jargon, and filled with practical examples, it will help you create amazing children's picture books.

That's enough about me, let's talk about you! So why do you want to write a Picture Book?

Here is a story I have heard all too often. Parents read picture books to their kids.

Their children love the stories and beg you to read it over and over again. After the millionth time, you think to yourself, this book is so simple, it is just some rhyming words and pictures. Anyone could write this. I'm going to write a picture book for my little Johnny.

And there you have it! Another hopeful picture book author is born.

The belief that writing a Picture Books is **EASY** is a common misconception. Picture books appear to be so simple, a basic plot or premise, simple language, fun illustrations of cuddly animals. How hard can it actually be?

The truth of the matter is, children's picture books are one of the most difficult genres to write for. Not only do you need to know what to write about and topics to avoid, but also how to fit your story into the rigid picture book format, how to write with the international market in mind, how to use language, theme and emotion to resonate with the target age of the reader.

This sounds very daunting, but you can do it! I tailored this book to show you everything you need to not only craft an awesome story but also how to format it, package it and submit it to literary agents or publishers.

This book follows the K.I.D.S principle,

KEEPING IT DELIGHTFULLY SIMPLE

So let's jump in and have some fun!

1. WHAT IS A PICTURE BOOK?

So, what is a picture book? There are many formats of picture books. They include board books, novelty books, early readers and the conventional picture book. The conventional picture book is the format we'll be focusing here.

At its core, a picture book is just that, it is a book containing pictures and minimal text.

The illustrations add another dimension to the text that creates a visual story experience unique to this style of book. Some standard norms are most picture books are usually 24 or 32 pages long, with 32 pages being the most popular.

They will just have one or two sentences on each page. In fact, the total word count should be between 200-500 words. Of course, there's always the exception to the rule, with some picture books having upwards of 1500 words. However, at the moment, the industry standard is between 200-500 words, with 300 being the sweet spot.

There are, however, two key elements a writer must adhere to. First, a picture book should contain a single theme or emotion that drives the story and second, the main character must solve the problem.

So, what makes a picture book special? The text: It's written with a beat or rhythm. The story doesn't have to rhyme, but it must hold a bounce, or a flow, kind of like a song.

The illustrations: can be simple illustrations or full visual narratives The way a picture book uses the text and illustrations together creates an experience that is greater than the illustrations or the text alone.

Using story elements like repetition, assonance and alliteration enhances the child's experience. In short, the picture book has something magical in between the text and the pictures.

A delightful picture book will engage the reader emotionally and mentally using well known universal themes like belonging, me growing up, loss, and bravery.

It will have a dominant topic or plot and will have engaging characters, something the child can believe in or empathise with. It will use good language structure. A great story needs to have conflict because, let's face it, without conflict, a story is boring.

It should be challenging, heart-warming, edgy, or at least leave the reader with a sense of hope. To sum it up in one line,

A **SINGLE** (Universal) **THEME** + over-riding **EMOTION** = Strong **COMPELLING STORY!**

Picture books are unique. While the text tells a specific story, the pictures should also tell a story. There are three styles of visual storytelling in picture books,

SYMMETRICAL (where the words and pictures match),

COMPLIMENTARY (where the illustrations enhance the story or add a sub story element) and,

CONTRADICTORY (where the words and pictures tell different stories but still create a cohesive story).

The aim of children's picture books is to create a shared experience between the child and parent, grandparent or carer. The adult reads the words, and the child follows along, looking at the pictures for added context. Remembering that the intended audience (children) cannot read themselves. As adults, we will often read a book once and then shelve it or give it away.

Not so with children, a well-constructed picture book, will have the child begging to read the story over and over again. This not only increases the value of the book but also demands that the quality of the book be far superior to other genres.

Definition: A picture book combines visual (illustrations) and verbal (text) stories in a book format, mainly aimed at young children.

Types of Picture Books:

Board books
These books, as the title describes, usually contain thick board pages with more interactive elements like texture elements, pop-ups or cut outs. Primarily designed to be read to babies, words are less important. They often contain a lot of actions and noises for the adult to read to the baby.

Concept books
These books aimed at the Toddler. They introduce basic learning of alphabet, numbers, colours and shapes. etc. They have more of an emphasis on words, however, pictures still get most of the toddlers' attention as they still rely on the adults to read the books.

Conventional picture books (This is the Style we will focus on)
These books aimed at the 4-6-year-old child need more of an entertaining story. They feature both words and pictures and can go up to 1500 words. However, the industry standard is between 200 - 500 words.

Easy readers
These are the next step up from early picture books they have a higher word count up to 2000 words. They use simple language and create conflict through action and dialogue. Written for the child to read them by themselves, they still feature illustrations on every page.

Page Count/Word Count

Traditionally accepted picture books are usually 24 or 32 pages. There are always the exception to the rules, but most publishing houses are looking for a 32 page book with between 200 - 500 words.

2. BEFORE WE START!

QUESTION 1. Do you have an idea for your story yet? If not, don't worry I will show you some awesome techniques for idea creation in the next chapter.

QUESTION 2. Do you know what style of character you want to create? Boy, girl, animal, alien, or even a monster. Why should the style of character be important?

QUESTION 3. Do you know what the problem is that the character must overcome?

In children's picture books, it is good practice to have a single emotional theme (problem) the main character needs to solve.

QUESTION 4. Do you know where the story is taking place? Story setting can be as important as character. You can change the entire story simply by changing the setting, environment, location or time period.

Sometimes as adults we forget kids respond to emotion. They see the world as it relates to them now. When thinking about writing for children, especially in the picture book genre, try to focus on:

What matters to kids?
Family and Friends
Games, School, Sharing
Animal, Hobbies, Interests
How they learn about the world
Feelings of Inclusion/Exclusion, Isolation, Love

What are kids scared of?
Monsters, the Dark, the Unknown
School, Bullies, Animals
Trouble at School/Home
Trouble with Friends
Feeling Alone, Sad, Different

Part One
****

It All Starts With...

3. IDEA CREATION

Everything starts with a killer idea. Easy enough! But where do these elusive ideas come from?

The most common question I get asked when doing school visits or author talks is how do you come up with the ideas for your stories? There are many ways to generate ideas, so let's go over some before we pick one for your story project.

Idea creation activity 1: **THE MAGIC OF KIDS**

Observing and talking with kids is one of the easiest and most fruitful ways to come up with story ideas. They are unfiltered and not constrained by adult beliefs. Often children voice their fantastical worlds, imaginary friends, darkest fears and nonsensical humour to anyone who will listen.

Keeping a notebook or digital recorder with you at all times helps to keep a record of these invaluable concepts as they arise.

Some examples of conversations I have had with kids include:

'Do zombies have to brush their teeth?'

'What are nits? Oh! OK, if they live in your hair, do they have tiny cities and schools?'

'If you put Big W, Bunnings, and Hungry Jacks together, would you have a Big Bunny Jack?'

'What's that dangly thing in your mouth? What does it do?'

Anyone of these would make a great and entertaining children's story... and yes, I am working on these very ideas as we speak.

Idea creation activity 2: *Every Day Events*

Another easy idea creation activity that everyone can do with or without kids is using an everyday event.

Step 1: make a list of as many everyday events as you can think of.

Eating breakfast	Going to school
Going to the shops	Going to bed
Building something	Playing with toys
Going to the beach	Going to the Zoo

Step 2: Take one or more of those everyday events and make something happen, create a problem, make it unusual.

Let's say we chose the everyday event of 'Going to bed'. Simple enough, our story begins with a child who is naughty and sent to bed early. During the night he is awakes to something rattling around in his room, there is a huge hairy figure towering over his toy pile. It is the Toy Taker. He has heard the stories but never believed them to be true. He thought they were just used to scare naughty kids.

But there the Toy Taker was, stuffing the boy's favourite toy in his satchel. The boy turns on his torch and shines it on the Toy Taker.

Step 3: Add a twist! Add something strange and unique to the event to make it engaging.

The Twist... The Toy Taker, frightened by the sudden interruption, stumbles into a pile of clothes. The boy smiles. He knows that if a child sees the Toy Taker; he has to give him all the toys in his satchel. The Toy Taker runs away screaming, tears streaming from his face as the boy settles back down to sleep, cuddling his pile of new toys.

Ok probably not the best moral for a children's story but it is funny, interesting and has the unexpected twist kids love.

Idea creation activity 3: FRACTURED FAIRY TALES

There is a huge revival of fairy tales in the children's book markets and no more so than the picture book genre.

Take an existing story and change it up. Change the principal character, change the time frame or period, change the antagonist or protagonist's role, change the point of view, or change the setting.

OK, let's examine how to do some of these:

Change the Main character: Jack and the Beanstalk. What if it wasn't Jack but Jane, and Jane wasn't just a girl but was a Ninja? Can you imagine where this story could go?

Change the time frame: Let's look at Alice in Wonderland, what if we set it in the very distant future, and instead of going down a rabbit hole, she travelled through a quantum portal. Just imagine the futuristic characters you could assign to each of the key players in this story.

Change the Antagonist/Protagonist: Can we do something with Peter Pan, a classic to be sure. What if, in reality, Peter was the bad guy, what if he was stealing the kids to work in his Neverland toy factory? Enter Captain Hook, a kind-hearted man determined to rescue the children and return them home. He lost his hand in the last battle with Peter Pan. Maybe the crocodile can be Captain Hook's pet. The possibilities are limitless.

Change the Point of view: One of my favourite examples of changing the point of view is Jon Scieszka The true story of the 3 little pigs' we hear the version of how A Wolf who had a terrible cold at the time went to his neighbours (who were the pigs) to borrow a cup of sugar, he didn't mean to blow their houses down, and they were already dead when he ate them, it was all just a big misunderstanding. You should really check it out. It is an outstanding example of this technique.

Change the setting: You can apply this to almost any story, it can be as simple as changing from a watery environment to the desert, or as complex as taking something like the Jungle Book story by Rudyard Kipling from the Indian forest and setting it all in space. Hey that's a pretty cool idea. I may have to explore that one myself.

Idea creation activity 4: *MATT'S 3 MAGIC BEANS*

One of my favourite techniques is using the 3 Essential Elements of a brilliant book. A Captivating Title, an Engaging Character and a Compelling Concept. Any of these in isolation can spark an idea for a great kid's book.

Instead of a high level theory of how to implement this approach, I wanted to give you the real-life examples that I used at the very beginning of my children's writing career.

USING THE TITLE:

One night my daughter, when she was still very young (about 2 years old) came outside to my wife and I and declared. 'There are monsters in my garden'. I sat with her and asked her what sort of monsters visited the garden? Were they friendly, or silly, clumsy or cool?

I wrote a rhyming story for her to include all her monsters, and we read it every night for over a year.

USING THE CHARACTER:

One day, while driving home from my son's day care, he informs me he is cranky! He then explains that it is not fair that I had written a book for his sister, but not him. I asked him if he wanted a story about his imaginary dinosaur friend Dun Dun. The smile that erupted on his face was priceless. So began my 2nd picture book. I took the one character 'Dun Dun' and constructed a funny romp through all the conceivable antics a child can get into trouble with and then blame on someone else.

Using a Concept:

My third technique is using a concept to build your story around. My kids really enjoyed 'Piranhas Don't Eat Bananas' written and illustrated by Aaron Blabey. The only problem was they weren't that keen on Piranhas. They wanted something that had Killer Whales in it.

I was interested in creating a book that could focus on healthy eating to raise awareness of the increased rate of childhood obesity in primary school children.

I took the concept of healthy eating and combined it with my kids' interest in killer whales and wrote my 4th picture book called 'A Killer Whale can't eat Kale!'

The story revolves around Doug, a killer whale who loves eating kale. The only problem is his friends don't like him eating all that healthy stuff. Written in rhyme, this hilarious story showcases how it is OK to be true to yourself and ignore peer pressure.

Doug tries to rescue the other animals from his friends by offering healthy alternatives. At the end of this book there is also a page dedicated to some STEM information on Killer Whales, their habitats, their diet and their size.

OK, let's give it a go. Using the following pages, see what ideas you can come up with for each ACTIVITY.

IDEA CREATION - ACTIVITY

1- Kids know what stories they love to read... Observing kids and talking to them can yield mountains of story ideas.

2 - Take everyday events, add a problem, add a twist and make it exciting.

3 - Change the principal character, change the time frame or period, change the antagonist or protagonist's role, change the point of view, or change the setting.

4 - A Captivating Title, an Engaging Character and a Compelling Concept.

4. CHARACTER CREATION

Creating your character is one of the most important steps in developing your story.

So what do we need to know about your character? In most instances, a picture book will have a single principal character. You can have more, but I recommend you don't exceed 3 major characters in your story, otherwise it becomes too difficult for the child to follow.

A well crafted character will endear themselves to a child even if it is not human, so how does this benefit you as the storyteller? When you create human characters for your story, you have to consider several other aspects. What gender, age and ethnicity will your character be?

For the most part, the characters can be interchangeable, and by that I mean human, animal, monster, alien or even an inanimate object like Thomas the Tank Engine by Reverend Wilbert Awdry.

What is the age of your character? A good rule of thumb is they should be within 1 to 2 years of the age of your target reader. More often than not, making the character slightly older than the reader is better, as it allows the child to imagine themselves as being able to do things older kids can do.

Most picture books rely on a single main character, because of the very minimal space we have to tell our stories having more than one main character can get confusing for the reader.

Okay, so why would you swap out human characters with animals, monsters, aliens or inanimate objects?

Having a non-human character helps your story appeal to everyone, it's just something to think about. Will your story still work if the main character was an animal, alien, monster, or object?

Let's move on, so what do you need to make an engaging character kids will love? First rule in character creation, make your character real. By this I mean nobody is perfect, and kids know this all too well. Remember, kids view the world as it relates to them now, and kids are smart and perceptive. They know they have traits and flaws. It is often the very thing that gets them in trouble, but also lets them have heaps of fun.

You want the reader (the child) to relate to your main character, empathise with them and maybe even emulate them to a point, so give them flaws and traits that make them less than perfect but super interesting.

Let's start with the name. If you don't already have a name, here's a really fun exercise you can do to create your character's name. It may even help you work out some of their traits. I learned this technique from the amazing Jen Storer queen of junior fiction.

Make a list of first names: you can search on Google or list all your friends and relatives, try to get around 20-30 names, write each one on a scrap piece of paper and put it in a container.

Then make a second list of last names you can think of and then write each one on a scrap piece of paper and put it in a second container.

Give both containers a good shake and then pull a piece of paper from the first name container and one from the second name container. Keep doing this until you have a combination that really sings to you. Sometimes you may want to just draw both names from the one container. There are no rules.

Once you have a name for your *HERO*, tell us more about them. What are their hobbies, interests, likes and dislikes; what emotional traits do they have; are they honest, creative, mischievous, or curious?

Children love to imagine themselves as the main character in the story they are reading, whether they are the hero, the scoundrel, the joker, it really doesn't matter. If the character is compelling, children will do this whether the character is a boy or a girl, an animal, an alien or even a monster.

Fill out the Character Design Sheet with as much detail as you can. You can always come back to it later and update as you get to know your **HERO** better.

CHARACTER TRAITS

active	excited	imaginative	quiet
adventurous	expert	jolly	quirky
affectionate	faithful	joyful	rational
alert	fair	joyous	reliable
ambitious	friendly	kind	responsible
bold	fun	lively	sensational
bright	funny	loving	sensible
brave	gentle	loyal	serious
calm	generous	mature	skilful
cheerful	good	mysterious	smart
clever	graceful	nice	shy
confident	grateful	noble	thankful
cool	groovy	nurturing	thoughtful
cooperative	happy	obedient	timid
courageous	hardworking	original	tireless
courteous	helpful	outgoing	trustworthy
curious	honest	peaceful	understanding
considerate	honourable	pleasant	useful
daring	hopeful	polite	victorious
dependable	humorous	popular	virtuous
determined	intelligent	popular	warm
eager	interesting	powerful	wilful
easy-going	introverted	proud	wordy
energetic	independent	quick	youthful

CHARACTER DESIGN SHEET

CHARACTER NAME

CHARACTER TYPE

EMOTIONAL TRAITS

PHYSICAL TRAITS

AGE

LIKES

DISLIKES

CLOTHING

ADDITIONAL THOUGHTS

WHAT DOES CHARACTER VALUE THE MOST?

WHAT DOES CHARACTER WANT MOST IN THE WORLD?

WHAT MUST CHARACTER DO TO GET IT?

CHARACTER DESIGN SHEET © MATT B LEWIS 2021

Part Two
****

Character Drives The Story

CHARACTER CREATION ACTIVITY

Sometime we get stuck in our heads with what the character should look like, or who they should be. They bombard us daily with every manner of marketing, from kids' books, comics, TV shows and movies.

So when it comes time to define your own character, it becomes so overwhelming that you end up with the dreaded...

Writer's Block

To help break out of this quandary I have come up with a fun little exercise called **Break That Stereotype**.

OK, so how does it work?

First pick a stereotype of a character you are thinking of having in your story. It could be a *Pirate*, an *Elf*, a *Troll* or a *Fairy* just to name a few. I have a Peter Pan fractured fairy tale I am working on, so I will use a fairy as my example.

Next, List all the characteristics and traits that make this character who they are. You can use the Character Design Sheet to help you identify each element for your chosen character.

Then swap out the obvious traits and attributes for something totally different. It can be silly, or functional, or outright impossible. It really doesn't matter, remember we are trying to break out of the learned stereotype, and allow our brains to create something unique and awesome.

Let's give it a go.

DAWN

Dawn is my Fairy: Age: 9

TRAITS
Helpful
Energetic
Fun
Happy
Busy
Secretive
Bossy
Unsure
Mischievous

OTHER
Tiny
Petite
Cute
Large Wings
Normal Skin colour
Clothes match nature
Wants to save nature
Scared of humans
Uses a wand

DONK

Donk is my Fairy Troll: Age: 9

TRAITS
Helpful
Shy
Lonely
Happy
Stubborn
Awkward
Clumsy
Unsure

OTHER
Huge
Dirty
Cute
Tiny Wings
Bluish Skin colour
Clothes Dirty Rags
Wants to be seen
Wants to be loved
Wears a utility pouch

Ok so let's see what this might look like if you were using the Character Design Sheet.

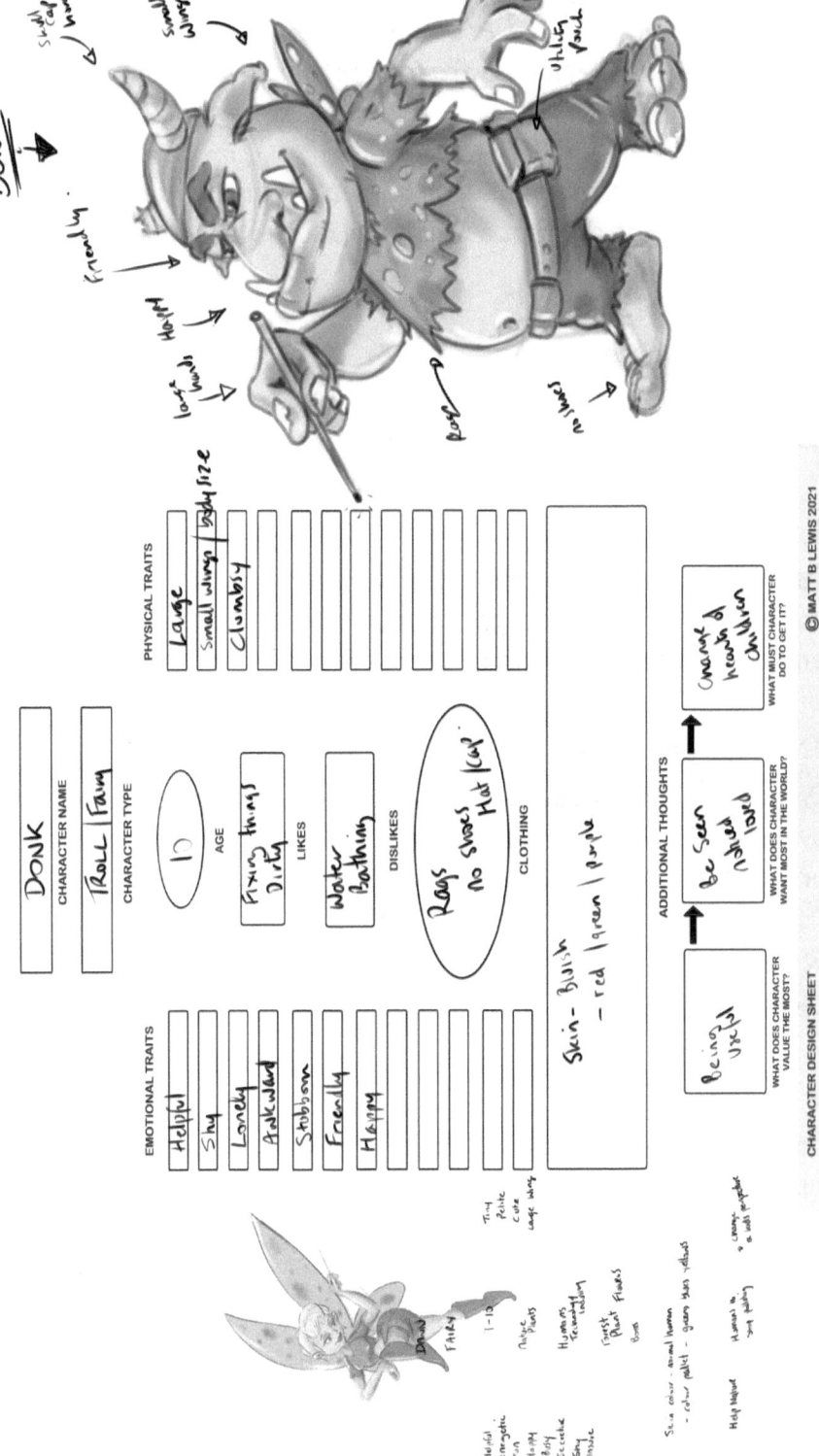

5. THE PLOT!
7 BASIC STORY PLOTS
(Analysis from Christopher Booker)

1. Overcoming the Monster

Definition: The protagonist or hero sets out to defeat an antagonistic or evil force which threatens them or their home/family, etc.

2. Rags to Riches

Definition: The poor protagonist gains power, wealth, and/or a mate, loses it all and gains it back, growing as a person.

3. The Quest

Definition: The protagonist and companions set out to gain an important object or to get to a location. They face temptations and other obstacles along the way.

4. Voyage and Return

Definition: The protagonist goes to a strange land and, after overcoming the threats it poses or learning important lessons unique to that location, they return with experience.

5. Comedy

Definition: Light and humorous character with a happy ending.

6. Tragedy

Definition: The protagonist is a hero with a major character flaw or great mistake, which is ultimately their undoing. Their unfortunate end often evokes pity.

7. Rebirth

Definition: An event forces the chief character to change their ways and often become a better individual.

IDEA: Think about your idea. Does it fit into any one plot?

CHARACTER: Think of your character: do they have any traits shown in any of the plots?

STORY: Think about the type of story, does it fall into any of the plots we've discussed?

Part Three
****

HOUSTON WE HAVE A PROBLEM!

6. THE PROBLEM!

Every story needs a central problem. As story creators, we need to come up with the **PROBLEM** and the **SOLUTION**, but it is crucial not to make the solution to your problem too predictable. Nothing bores a reader more than knowing exactly what is going to happen in the first few pages, or knowing how little Johnny Black will solve the obvious problem.

So get creative and be innovative. There is really only one rule you MUST abide by, and that is the main character or hero MUST solve the problem. No one else can solve it (no parents, or secondary characters, it has to be the main character!).

OK, so little Johnny must solve the problem, but there's nothing to say how crazy or left of centre that solution can be.

Let's look at little Johnny Blank, he's always being bullied on his way home from school - so the primary emotion here is **FEAR**, fear of being bullied. This story would fit into the overcoming the monster plot. The bullies represent the **MONSTER**.

Now that you have identified the main **PROBLEM**, you need to create 3 or more obstacles for your Hero to encounter, before resolving the key problem.

Let's have little Johnny Blank leaving school early to avoid the bullies, but they see him and throw him in a dumpster. That's obstacle 1.

Next, little Johnny Blank tries staying back after school, but they're waiting for him near the shops and throw milk shakes over him. That's obstacle 2.

Then one afternoon on his way home, little Johnny Blank hears a scary noise, he goes towards it to see what it is. This is his first step in overcoming his fears. He sees a giant, scruffy English Mastiff with this foot stuck in the storm drain.

The dog is snarling and scary (this is obstacle 3), but little Johnny Blank wants to help him. It is part of his character trait; he is courageous, caring and helpful. Johnny Blank gives the dog his sandwich and frees his foot. The dog becomes a happy pup and prances around Johnny Blank.

This time on his way home, the bullies jump out from behind a hedge to rough Johnny up, but the English Mastiff jumps in between them, snarling.

The bullies run away crying, and Little Johnny Blank and his new best friend play together all the way home. The story could end with a clean and pampered dog sleeping on little Johnny Blank's bed with his new collar that says Angus.

This is not the expected solution, and granted, it could use a little finesse, but it serves the purpose of the thinking of an unexpected way to solve a problem.

Another thing to consider when creating your problem is not to rush through the problem, even though we only have a few pages to tell our story. You need to dwell on the problem. There needs to be a struggle. The hero needs to have several attempts at solving the problem before they are successful.

Look at every movie you've ever watched... Do you know the solution in the first 10 minutes, or do they drag it out to the very end?

Present different ways the character can attempt to solve the problem. Little Johnny tried leaving early, tried staying late and tried going home a different way, but still encounter the bullies at every turn.

There could be three or four different attempts at trying things before your **HERO** gets the right solution, but don't make it too easy or predictable.

THE IDEAL SOLUTION WILL ALWAYS BE A SURPRISE AND HAVE A TWIST!

YOUR PROBLEM NOW!

OK, it's your turn. If you are struggling with what problem the principal character needs to solve, remember the list in chapter one that focused on kids' fears (isolation, bullies, feeling different etc.). I've listed it below gain for you to review.

Depending on your setting (space, future, ancient times, earth, monster universe etc.). The problems can be quite different. Just remember to focus it on one primary emotion.

Whatever the problem, no matter how complex or difficult it is to overcome, there is one rule you must follow... The main character **MUST** solve it themselves.

Pick a single **THEME** or **EMOTION** for your character to overcome!

WHAT MATTERS TO KIDS?
Family and Friends
Games, School, Sharing
Animal, Hobbies, Interests
How they learn about the world
Feelings of Inclusion/Exclusion, Isolation, Love

WHAT ARE KIDS SCARED OF?
Monsters, the Dark, the Unknown
School, Bullies, Animals
Trouble at School/Home
Trouble with Friends
Feeling Alone, Sad, Different

THEME

EMOTION

7. BUILD YOUR WORLD!

Okay, so now we have our **CHARACTER**, we have a **PROBLEM** for them to solve, we now need a **WORLD** for the story to occupy. The world that you create can be a realistic world. You can set it on Earth, in a town, on a farm, or any location that we're all familiar with.

We see many picture books set in the real world, but we can also set them somewhere else! By changing the environment, you can change the entire story. I discussed this in one of the earlier lessons when I used Alice in Wonderland as an example. If I were to take this story and set it in the far distant future, and instead of going down a rabbit hole, she goes through a quantum portal, how would this change the story? It would be a different universe with different creatures, and even though the creatures look different, they would still occupy the same character roles as the original story.

You can see how the original story will start off with the same plot. However, being set in a completely unique environment it gives you the opportunity to have the story take a tangent or divert into another path where you can change that story completely. This is a good thing because Children like to have things that are interesting and unique.

If you're going to go down the path of creating a universe, a world, or setting your story on a different planet, you have many options. It can be a planet in our solar system, or a made up planet that nobody's ever heard of, a planet that's just for monsters or a world of fish. It doesn't really matter, wherever you decide to set your story, there needs to be elements that ground the story in the real world now, because remember, children see and engage in the world as it relates to them now.

So if you set something into fantastical and too far out, that doesn't have any relevance to our world today, it might just be too abstract for a child to understand.

So what do I mean by this? Okay, I'm currently working on a story for my youngest kid called Fred Lice. Now Fred is a boy who has head lice, but his head lice are his friends. The entire story takes place in the hair on his head. There will be buildings and schools and vehicles made of scalp tissue, oils and hair.

Even though this is all make believe **KIDS** can still relate to it, they know what cities, transport, schools, and holidays are.

No matter where you are setting your story, whether you set in an underwater world or a space chasm or a monster universe, go over your storey and see if you can identify the elements that relate back to the current world. It is critical to keep some point of reference that the child or the reader can refer to and understand what you are trying to say.

This is still a world. It has buildings or schools; It has vehicles or some transport; it has the same problems we have in our world now, like pollution, food shortages, or bullies.

Your world might have monsters and many strange and exotic things, but it still needs to refer or relate back to the world that we currently live in.

So your **ACTIVITY** will be to take your idea or story so far, and write **WHEN** and **WHERE** it will take place.

Remember to list elements that help ground the story in the child's current reality.

Every story needs to live

SOMEWHERE!

Where you decide to create your world impacts how the reader will perceive your story. Remember that in order for kids to relate to your world and understand your story, it needs to be grounded with real world elements.

Where will your story take place?
Is it set on earth, if so, in which country, city or street name?
What if you set it in space, or on a distant planet, or another universe, or altered reality all together?

When will your story take place?
Describe the timeline. Is it set in the Past | Present | or future?

Combine both elements to create a new world.
(Example: Perhaps you have chosen the Old West, set on a different planet, where the inhabitants are not human.)

8. THE 3 ACTS

The 3 Act Structure is the story structure that is most common to every story ever written. Many people think that the 3 Act Structure doesn't apply to picture books, and there are some picture books out there that don't follow a plot or 3 Act Structure.

One that comes to mind is the hairy McClary books, a lot of fun, and they don't really follow a plot, but as a general rule, most books, including picture books, follow the 3 Act Structure. OK, that's great, but what is the 3 Act Structure? Simply put, it's a story that contains a start, a middle and an end.

Act one is the start where you introduce the hero and the problem. Act Two is the middle where the hero has to overcome multiple challenges or obstacles before reaching the climax, and
Act Three is the end, where the action falls off to a resolution and happy ending or feeling of hope.

In larger stories like movies, plays or novels with 60000 plus words, they break the 3 Act Structure down into 25% for this first act, 50% for the second act and 25% for the third act. In picture books, we only have between 20 to 28 pages to tell our story. So I work on a 15%-70%-15% rule. This is my personal observations and what works well for me, but you can vary this as required.

The goal is to introduce the action as soon as possible, preferably by page four, and then have most of the book tell the middle of a story or Act Two and then finish up quickly with the resolution.

So, let's have a look at what the 3 Act Structure really looks like. We first introduce our character and then something happens to that character, a call of action to make them have to do something.

Then the action of the story rises, the character faces a challenge or an obstacle they have to overcome, often they fail, then they have another obstacle to overcome again, often failing, but they keep trying.

Most of the time there will only be three challenges, but they can have six or seven challenges before they get to the interlude or turning point. The realisation, where they find a clue that will help them with their major problem. Finally, they reach the climax or ultimate battle, defeat the foe or work out the solution, or solve the mysteries of the world.

After the climax, there is a sharp drop (falling action) that leads to a resolution and a return to the status quo.

Okay, so that's fine. I've covered the technical aspect of the 3 Act Structure, so let's have a look at how it pertains to a well-known story by Julia Donaldson the Gruffalo.

I think everybody on the planet has either read the story, had the story read to them, or at the very least seen the movies? It's a wonderful story and beautifully illustrated by Axel Scheffler.

The story starts with a mouse going for a stroll in the deep, dark woods. This introduces the character and the problem (he's hungry looking for a nut to eat).

Then something happens. 'A fox sees the mouse, and the mouse looks good'. The mouse knows the fox wants to eat him. This is the first challenge he has to get away from the fox.

So, he tells him the story about the Gruffalo which scares the fox off, problem one avoided.

Then something happens, 'an owl sees the mouse, and the mouse looks good', our hero tells the owl about the Gruffalo which scares him off. Problem two avoided.

Then something happens, 'a snake sees the mouse, and the mouse looks good', our hero tells the snake about the Gruffalo which scares him off. Problem three avoided.

Now our **HERO** meets the biggest problem, the Gruffalo, who wants to eat him, so he tricks the Gruffalo into thinking he is the scariest creature in the woods. This leads to a reversal of the first three challenges.

On the return trip, he meets the snake, and the Gruffalo terrifies the snake so he slithers away.

Then Meets the owl, the owl sees the Gruffalo and flies away.

The final meeting is with the fox, the fox sees the Gruffalo and runs away.

Then the mouse has an epiphany, a realisation, or turning point, the mouse says to the Gruffalo, 'see everyone is afraid of me'.

This is the pivotal point of the story where the main character (the Mouse) takes ownership of the problem and comes up with a unique solution. He scares the Gruffalo by telling him he's hungry for Gruffalo crumble.

This leads to the climax with the Gruffalo running away.

Finally, to a quick resolution where the mouse finds a nut, and the nut was good.

By following the basic **3 ACT STRUCTURE** with the 32 page layout, we can map out the major events for our story relatively quickly.

Let's give it a go!

Remember, almost **EVERY** story **EVER** told fits into the 3 ACT Structure

3 ACT STRUCTURE

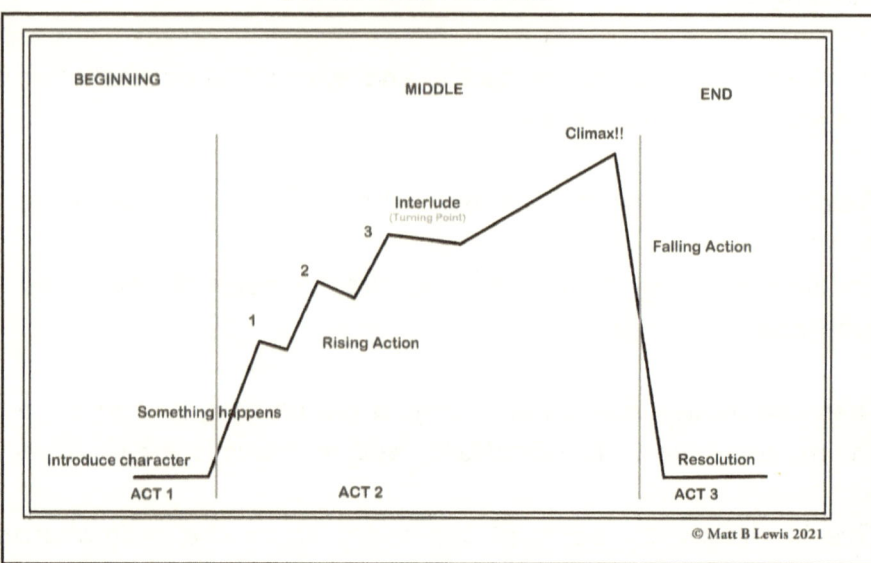

Most stories work on the 25|50|25 rule that is 25% ACT 1, 50% ACT 2 and 25% ACT 3.

As Picture Books only have 24-28 pages for the story, I use the 15/70/15 rule.
- Introduce character page 3 or 4
- The next 21 pages cover ACT 2
- The last 3 pages for happy ending - feeling of hope.

ACT 1: introduce the main character/protagonist and the problem.

40

ACT 2: the protagonist faces 3 challenges (often failing at each), they reach a turning point where the protagonist works out how to solve the problem, there is a climax where they often succeed.

ACT 3: The action slows to a happy ending or a feeling **of hope.**

Part Four
✳✳✳✳✳✳✳✳✳✳✳

To Tell A Good Yarn

9. TELL A GOOD STORY

So what are the important elements of storytelling? There are many tools that you can use to improve the beat and flow of your story and increase reader engagement. They are:
- Rhyming, rhythm and repetition,
- Alliteration, Assonance, and Onomatopoeia
- Rule of Threes, Emotions, and Show Don't Tell

There is an age-old question with kids' picture books, and that is, do I write in Rhyme?

To answer this, you should first ask yourself, 'will it improve my book?' The simple fact is, rhythm or the beat of the story is more important than rhyme.

Traditional publishers prefer new authors to write in Prose (the text doesn't rhyme). There are many reasons for this. One I hear all the time is: rhyming stories don't translate well for the international market. This is usually the default answer from publishers and agents. It allows them to use the excuse that it limits the market they can publish to, which reduces their ability to recover the costs of royalty advances, marketing, etc. In most cases, publishers don't like rhyming stories because people simply do it poorly. And let's be honest here, in most cases, you won't know if an editor or publisher doesn't like your story because it's in rhyme. You simply won't get a response at all.

When using rhyme, one of the biggest mistakes emerging writers make and one I have made once or twice myself, is to force the rhyming of words at the expense of a good story arc.

Rhyming is an art form; it isn't just a matter of matching words at the end of a sentence. There are so many other factors to consider, such as the metre, the stress on syllables, the syllable count and the number of lines per stanza, to mention just a few.

But for all those avid poets among us (including me) let's have a look at writing in RHYME.

Using ELEMENTS of good writing to make your book SING!

RHYME

The simple fact is rhythm (or the beat of the story) is more important than rhyme. But if you are going to write in rhyme, here's what you need to know.

RHYME is made up of individual units called **FEET**, which have a *specific number of syllables* and a *specific pattern of emphasis*.

The most common types of metrical feet are two syllables and three syllables long. They're characterised by their particular combination of stressed syllables and unstressed syllables.

They include:
- Trochee. Pronounced DUH-duh, as in "ladder."
- Iamb. Pronounced duh-DUH, as in "indeed."
- Spondee. Pronounced DUH-DUH, as in "TV."
- Dactyl. Pronounced DUH-duh-duh, as in "certainly."
- Anapaest. Pronounced duh-duh-DUH, as in "what the heck!" (Anapaestic poetry typically divides its stressed syllables across multiple words.)

The rhythmic feet are repeated over the course of a line of poetry to create poetic meter. The length of this meter uses Greek terminology.
- one foot = monometer
- two feet = dimeter
- three feet = trimeter
- four feet = tetrameter
- five feet = pentameter
- six feet = hexameter
- seven feet = heptameter
- eight feet = octameter

Write a couple of 4 line stanzas in rhyme: Then go over them and work out how many syllables are in each and what the Metrical foot is.

Here is an example of a Dactylic Pentameter:
**What is a Twickle? I'm searching for clues.
What do they look like, and where do they snooze?**

What is a Twickle? I'm searching for clues.
| | | | || | || | |
What do they look like, and where do they snooze?
| | | | | | | | | |

MAKE YOUR STORY SING!

OK, so whether you decide to write in *RHYME* or *PROSE*, the focus of your writing should be on creating a *BEAT* or *RHYTHM*. Writing a Picture Book is like writing a *SONG*.

How many songs do you know where you can sing the chorus, but then you hum the verses (because you forget the words). We know the chorus because they repeat it so many times throughout the song, where the verses usually only occur once or twice. The chorus also has a distinctive rhythm that resonates with the listener, making them want to join in.

This is the same for picture books. Whenever a child can read or listen to the story and they are able to repeat the core sections of that story, it increases engagement and enjoyment in the story.

So how can we achieve this in our writing? I use:

THE RULE OF 3'S
REPETITION
ALLITERATION
ASSONANCE, AND
ONOMATOPOEIA.

I know it sounds like a lot, but once you understand the basics, it will become second nature in your writing.

So let's look at each one, and have a practice at incorporating it into our story.

RULE of 3's

The rule of 3's refers to introducing 3 things in a row that helps create a repetitive beat. They can be sound effects like:

Clink, Clank, Clunk.
Bing, Bang, Bonk.

They can be activities like meeting 1st character, a 2nd character, then a 3rd character.

They can be language structure like:

Deep Dark Night

Or even character names.

Big Bunny Jack

The Gruffalo by Julia Donaldson is a superb example of the rule of 3's

Three characters
The fox, the owl and the snake

Three activities
Meeting each character

Three groups of three descriptions.
Terrible tusks, terrible claws, terrible teeth in terrible jaws

Three meetings after the turning point

Character name
'Little brown mouse,'

Language structure
'Goodbye little mouse,'; 'deep dark woods,'

Make a list of sound effects

CRASH
BANG
SWISH
WALLOP

Make a list of character names

AJAX
ABERNATHY
PETA
BONEVENTURE
ERIC
MATTHEWS
DERRICK
DUFFY

Make a list of repetitive language

DEEP DANK FORREST

TEENY WEENY TADPOLE

"HELLO MR WILD"

RAZOR SHARP CLAWS

ALLITERATION

Alliteration happens when words that start with the same sound (not just the same letter) repeat in a phrase or sentence. The sound is usually a consonant and the words don't have to be right next to one another.

Peter pepper picked peaches by the placid puddle

ASSONANCE

Assonance is a literary device in which the repetition of similar vowel sounds takes place in two or more words in proximity to each other within a line of poetry or prose. Assonance most often refers to the repetition of internal vowel sounds in words that do not end the same.

Son of a gun
Motion of the ocean
Stranger danger.

ONOMATOPOEIA

Onomatopoeia is when a word describes a sound and actually mimics the sound of the object or action it refers to when spoken. It is also where you use words that sound like the action-sound effect words.

The Bees Buzzed
Cock-a-Doodle-Doo
Splat, Clang, Whoosh

ALLITERATION

ASSONANCE

ONOMATOPOEIA

REPETITION

Kids may not understand all the words in a Picture Book, but once they see and hear the pattern, rhythm or beat of the repetition, they're hooked and you'll see them light up when they get to say the words. Examples:

The Three Little Pigs:
Little pig, little pig let me in...
Not by the hair on my chinny chin chin.

I'll huff and I'll puff and I'll blow your house in.

Going On a Bear Hunt:
kids love to repeat the chorus...

'We can't go over it,
we can't go under it,
oh no we'll have to go through it.'

Repetition can be used for sound effects too and if you combine it with alliteration (words starting with the same letter) and the rule of 3's then you can produce some powerful story beats that will have the kids chanting along.

Splish, Splash, Splosh
Bing, Bang, Bong.

My kids absolutely loved doing the sound effects in every book they read... even as they transition into chapter books and graphic novels.

REPEAT, REPEAT, REPEAT

Time to practise. In the spaces below, write the actions that repeat, sounds that repeat, or phrases that repeat.

Don't worry about being too perfect, let your mind run with it and have fun!

SHOW DON'T TELL

Show don't tell is the art of allowing the reader to experience the story through action, words, thoughts, senses, and feelings. Using descriptive phrase we can provide a better experience for the reader and provide them with the opportunity to make their own interpretations.

With the limited word count and pages in picture books, this has never been more important. Here is a quick example of show vs tell.

TELLING
Tempest walked along the beach and saw seagulls and tourists getting food.

SHOWING
The wet sand squelched through her toes. She could smell the hot chips and hear the seagulls nattering as they swooped on unsuspecting tourists.

Now, which do you think will have the kids' imagination more engaged?

Choose one of the following prompts or think of your own emotion or adjective. Take fifteen minutes to write a piece that shows us that feeling.

SADNESS
ANGER
FEAR
SURPRISE
JOY
EXCITEMENT
KINDNESS

Revise your work and look for adjectives or feelings. These words can reveal when you're telling, and not showing.

Example: Anger.

TELLING: She was angry.

SHOWING: Tempest stormed off and slammed her door shut.

EMOTIONAL RESONANCE

Emotion is the key element in picture books that keeps the reader engaged. It is emotion which drives the story, and at the risk of repeating myself, the big emotion and the theme in each picture book story should be the same thing.

A picture book should only have one emotion or one theme.

No matter what emotion you want your scene to have, it has to feel real. The best way to achieve that is to write something that brings out that emotion in you.
What terrifies you, what excites you, what makes you sad, silly or angry?

EMOTIONAL RESONANCE EXERCISE

STEP 1: Write a list of as many emotions as you can think of. (Or just Google some)

- Admiration
- Adoration
- Aesthetic
- Appreciation
- Amusement
- Anger
- Anxiety
- Awe
- Awkwardness
- Boredom
- Calmness
- Confusion
- Craving
- Disgust
- Desire
- Empathy
- Entrancement
- Excitement
- Fear
- Horror
- Interest
- Joy
- Jealous
- Annoyed
- Nostalgia
- Relief
- Romance
- Sadness
- Satisfaction
- Surprise

STEP 2 write a list of everyday events. (Try to come up with 5 - 10)

- Eating breakfast
- First day at school
- Going to the shops
- Going to bed
- Getting a new toy
- Going to the zoo

STEP 3 Pair an event with an emotion from Step 2 (Example: Getting a new toy + Excitement)

EVENT	EMOTION

STEP 4 Brainstorm or Mind Map all the activities that could happen when getting a new toy that makes a character feel excitement?

ACTIVITIES	EMOTION

STEP 5 Rinse and Repeat

Next try using the same event but pick a different emotion.

EVENT	EMOTION

Or, how about using the same emotion but pick a different event.

EVENT	EMOTION

10. TIME TO WRITE

OK, so you finally get to WRITE!

Using the techniques from Chapter 3, write the idea you have come up with for your story.

IDEA

Now let's write all the traits you came up with for your character. Feel free to sketch it out if it helps

CHARACTER

What is the main THEME or EMOTION, what PROBLEM does your character need to overcome?

PROBLEM

WHEN and WHERE is your Story taking place?

YOUR WORLD

Now it's time to work out how your story fits into a 32 page book.

OK, so if you remember my picture book formula of 15%-70%-15% we need to introduce our HERO and the PROBLEM in the first 15% of the book.

With a 32 page picture book the 1st page is normally the Half-Title page, the 2nd page is the Copyright/Dedication Page and the 3rd page is the TITLE page, sometime I swap the Title and Half-Title pages around. This leaves us with 28 pages for the story and illustrations. In some books you can lose the Half-Title page and end up with 30 pages, but more often than not work on having 28 usable pages.

We can use the 32 page template to work out where each part of the story needs to occur.

Introduce the character by page 4, Introduce the problem by page 6, pages 8-9 first obstacle, pages 12-13 second obstacle, pages 16-17 third obstacle, pages 20-23 epiphany learns something, pages 24-27 climax, pages 28-29 resolution, pages 30-31 happy ending.

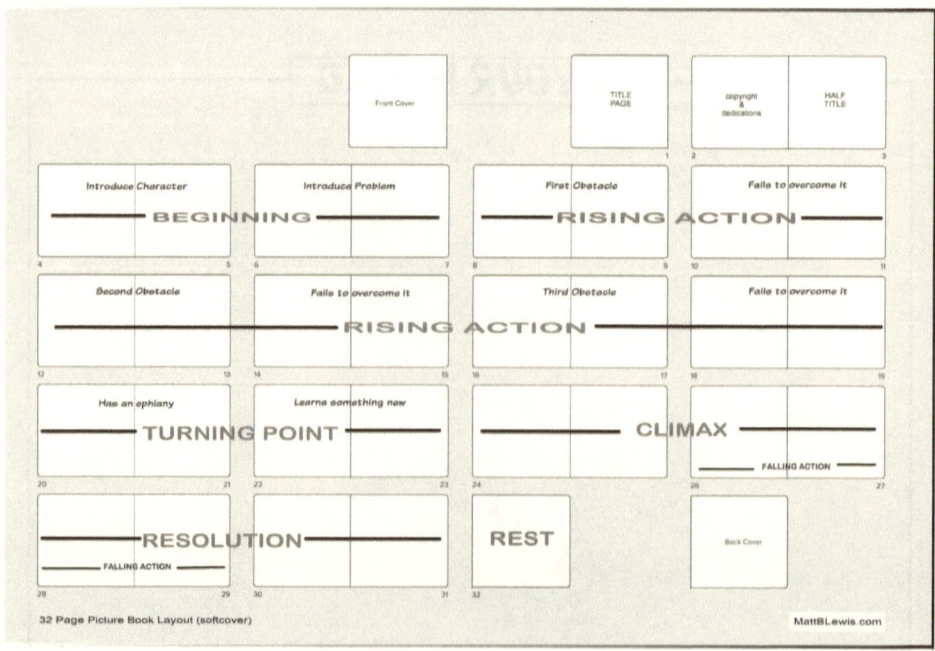

PAGE LAYOUT

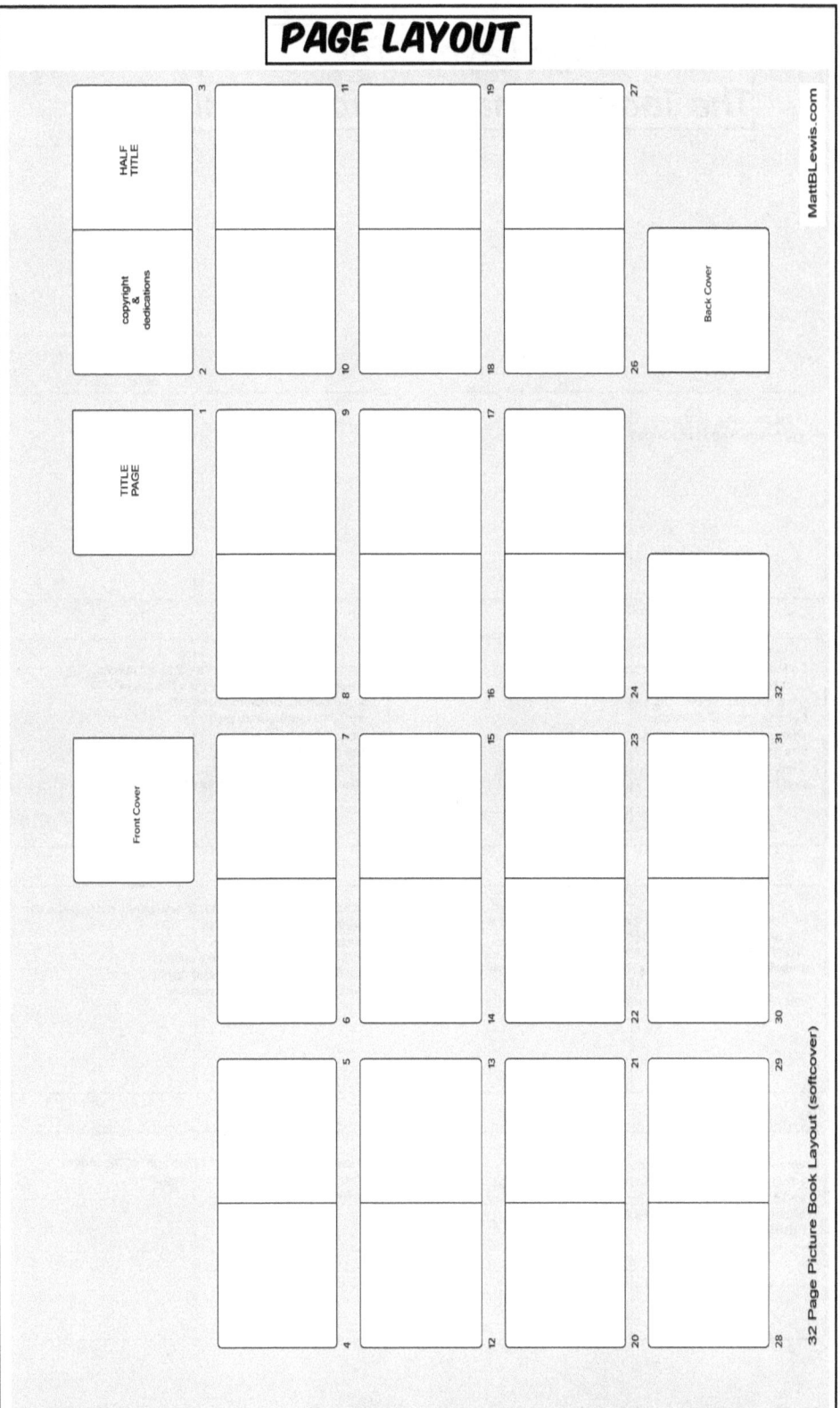

Page Layout for The Tadpole That Ate Too Much!

Front Cover

---

4 — In the morning, as the sun warmed the water, the egg hatched and out popped…

5

6 — A Teeny Weeny Tadpole.

7

---

12 — On Monday morning she saw 1 piece of algae float by, 'CHOMP!' she gobbed it up 'That tastes horrible' she said. But she was still starving. Then something happened. She grew a leg. 'That's strange!' said the tadpole.

13

14 — On Tuesday morning she saw 2 small leaves, 'They have to taste better than the algae' she thought. 'CHOMP! MUNCH!' she gobbled them up they were tough to swallow, and she was still starving. Then she grew another leg. How weird!' said the tadpole?

15

---

20 — On Friday morning, 5 fat dragonflies landed on the water. She jumped out and. 'CHOMP! MUNCH, GULP! CRUNCH! SQUISH!' she gobbled them up 'Delicious!' said the tadpole, but she was still starving, and now she had this huge sticky tongue that wouldn't stay in her mouth.

21

22 — On Saturday morning with her new sticky tongue she ate 1 long leech, 1 slow shrimp, 1 wriggling worm, 1 fat fly, 1 cranky caterpillar, 1 scary spider, 1 brittle beetle, 1 giant grasshopper, 1 tiny turtle, and 1 mighty mouse.

23

---

28 — When the sun rose on Sunday, she was no longer a teeny weeny tadpole. She had four muscular legs and a long sticky tongue. She was a big, beautiful FROG. RIBBIT!

29

30 — One cool summer's night, by the light of the moon, a big beautiful FROG lay seven eggs on the surface of a pond.

31

---

32 Page Picture Book Layout (softcover)

1 TITLE PAGE

2 copyright & dedications

3 One cool summer's night, by the light of the moon, a lonely egg lay on the surface of a pond.

8 Frightened and alone, her tummy grumbled. 'I'm starving,' she said as she swam around looking for something to eat.

9

10 'I'm so Teeny Weeny, what can I eat?'

11

16 On Wednesday morning she saw something different in the water, 3 squiggly, wriggly mosquito larvae, 'They look Yummy' said the tadpole, 'CHOMP! MUNCH! GULP!' she gobbled them up she was still starving and what's worse, she grew a third leg. 'Why does this keep happening?' said the tadpole.

17

18 On Thursday morning she found 4 water striders. They were fast, but her muscular legs made her faster and, 'CHOMP! MUNCH, GULP! CRUNCH!' she gobbled them up 'Wow crunchy' said the tadpole. She was still starving and then she grew a fourth leg. 'Oh well' said the tadpole.

19

24 She was no longer starving. 'OUCH! My tummy hurts' said the tadpole.

26 So she lay on a lily pad and drifted off to sleep. While she was sleeping, she didn't notice one last change. Her tail fell off! 'PLOP!'

27

32 STEM SHEET

Back Cover

MattBLewis.com

Before we write our first draft, we need to take everything we have worked on so far and create a rough outline of **WHAT** happens **WHEN**.

Quickly fill in the following sections:
Have you worked out a title for your Picture Book yet?

TITLE

IDEA

CHARACTER

PROBLEM

YOUR WORLD

WHEN:

WHERE:

THE OUTLINE

In one or two lines write down the actions you see occurring on each page spread.

Title:

Page 4-5:

Page 6-7:

Page 8-9:

Page 10-11:

Page 12-13:

Page 14-15:

Page 16-17:

Page 18-19:

Page 20-21:

Page 22-23:

Page 24-25:

Page 26-27:

Page 28-29:

Page 30-31:

Page 32:

OK, how did you go filling out your outline? My story looks like this:

IDEA: Life cycle of a Frog
CHARACTER: Tadpole
TITLE: The Tadpole That Ate Too Much
PROBLEM: Starving Where Can She Find Food?
THE WORLD: A Pond

> **Page 3** Introduce tadpole (the egg)
>
> **Page 4-5:** Egg hatches, she's starving - eats something
>
> **Page 6-7:** Grows a leg
>
> **Page 8-9:** Still starving - eats something
>
> **Page 10-11:** Grows a second leg
>
> **Page 12-13:** Still starving - eats something
>
> **Page 14-15:** Grows a third leg
>
> **Page 16-17:** Still starving - eats something
>
> **Page 18-19:** Grows a fourth leg
>
> **Page 20-21:** Still starving - eats something
>
> **Page 22-23:** Gets a long sticky tongue
>
> **Page 24-25:** Eats many creatures
>
> **Page 26-27:** Too full, sore stomach - falls asleep
>
> **Page 28-29:** Tail falls off - no longer tadpole
>
> **Page 30-31:** Turns into a FROG
>
> **Page 32:** STEM sheet - Information on Frogs and Toads

11. YOUR FIRST DRAFT

Let's put everything together and write our first draft. One important aspect I have found for writing the first draft is to just go for it! Don't edit yourself or be too perfect. Let the creativity flow, regardless if you are writing in *RHYME* or *PROSE*.

Look at your outline and write one or two sentences for each. Try to have an action word in line and remember the primary *EMOTION* or *THEME* you have selected for your story.

EXAMPLE:
Page 3 Introduce tadpole as an egg...

One cool summer's night, by the light of the moon, a little egg lay on the surface of a pond.

This sentence sets up the *WHEN*, (it is night-time), *WHERE* we are in a pond (as that is the most likely environment for tadpoles) and the *WHAT* or *WHO* an egg

Like I mentioned earlier, don't try to over analyse every sentence at this stage, just write out your thoughts for each action you created in your outline.

For those who want to write in rhyme, it could read:

On a cool summer night, by the light of the moon,
Lay an egg that was hoping to hatch very soon.

(Anapaest Hexameter)

This is just a quick example that I literally wrote for this example, with no real thought of scheme or placement. But it highlights what I mean by not over analysing your writing at this stage.

FIRST DRAFT

1. One cool summer's night, by the light of the moon, a little egg lay on the surface of a pond.

2. On Sunday morning, as the sun warmed the pond, something emerged from the egg. A teeny, weeny tadpole.

3. She was starving, so she swam around looking for something to eat.

4. On Monday she ate 1 piece of algae and grew one leg, but she was still starving.

5. On Tuesday she ate 2 small leaves and grew a second leg, but she was still starving.

6. On Wednesday she ate 3 mosquito larvae and grew a third leg, but she was still starving.

7. On Thursday she ate 4 water striders and grew a fourth leg, but she was still starving.

8. On Friday she ate 5 dragonflies. Oh, no, her tail dropped off, and she was still starving.

9. On Saturday she ate 1 long leech, 1 slow shrimp, 1 wriggling worm, 1 fat fly, 1 cranky caterpillar, 1 scary spider, 1 brittle beetle, 1 giant grasshopper, 1 weeny turtle, and 1 mighty mouse.

10. That night she had a tummy ache. So she lay on a lily pad and fell asleep.

11. She was no longer a teeny, weeny tadpole. With four muscular legs and a huge sticky tongue. She was a big, beautiful FROG.

12. One cool summer's night, by the light of the moon, she lay seven eggs.

Let's take a quick segue and discuss *OUTLINING* versus *SEAT OF YOUR PANTS* or SOP for writing your first draft.

There is an ongoing debate between the merits of being a *PLOTTER* or *PANTSER*. The truth of the matter is, it doesn't really matter which technique you choose, as long as you get a brain dump down for your initial draft. Because let's face the truth, it is easier to edit horrible writing than a blank page! I really had to tone that saying down for this book...ha ha haaa!

Out of the multitude of picture books I have written, I have used both techniques with outstanding success. So why have I chosen to show the outlining method in this book and not the SOP technique? Well, there is no real technique to the Seat of Your Pants writing, you just go with the flow and write what comes to you with little thought of where it fits into the larger story arc initially, it is only at the rewrite stage do you then have to figure out where everything fits and if you need to add more back story or remove extraneous information.

The reason I showed the outlining technique is simple. In most cases, an emerging picture book writer will spend days, weeks, even months crafting their wonderful story. They made it sound beautiful, used excellent rhyming, but have forgotten one core element. The Story! Or plot. It is easy to write a story that introduces a character and then lots happen on the pages between, but it doesn't follow a story arc, the character doesn't solve a problem and there is no real resolution.

There are plenty of fun picture books out there that do not follow a plot, but in most cases an editor or publisher will want a well-structured plot, where they can see the character grow through the 3 Acts and discover a wonderful and/or surprising conclusion.

OK, back to writing your first draft. However you want to create it.

REVIEWING YOUR FIRST DRAFT

CONGRATULATIONS! You've written your first draft.

Sincerely, well done! That is often the most daunting step. To overcome your own self-doubt (and believe me, I have been there too) is an awesome achievement that you should be proud of!

Now for the fun part, how do we turn this flurry of chaotic rambling into a polished children's story that kids (and publishers) will love.

STEP 1: Put the story away for as long as you can stand it. A day, a week, even a few weeks. I know it sounds crazy, but the longer you can leave it, the better. Looking at your story with a fresh set of eyes will greatly improve your revisions.

STEP 2: Read through your story in its entirety, then read it aloud, or have someone read it to you (or you can record yourself reading it and then play it back) - this step is very important if you write in rhyme.

Does the story flow, when you listen to the story, does it make sense? Are there any spots where you think something is missing? Look at the word choices you made. Are you telling the reader about what is happening or are you showing them?

STEP 3: Read through your story again. This time, look at your structure to see how it fits into the 3 Acts.
- Does your introduction invoke curiosity in the reader?
- Does the action/problem start early in your story?
- Do you use one of the five senses on each page?
- Did you tell a story?
- If writing in rhyme are the stanzas of a consistent length?

STEP 4: Using the notes from all these questions, revisit your story. Read each line and see where you can strengthen it. Now rewrite your story!

Let's have a quick look at an example of editing your story. This is the 3rd story I ever wrote back in 2017. Look at the critical issues.

INTRO CHARACTER ✓ **33 GRAMMAR ISSUES** **UNREALISTIC VISUAL**

Deep inside a wooden hollow, all warm and safe and snug,
There lives a ~~baby cockatoo~~ no ~~larger than a bug~~,
His plumage black, his tail is red, and short or somewhat stocky,
But that's ok he's perfect still and known as simply OCKY.

CLUMSY WORDING TO MAKE LINE LENGTH

Outside a FRENZIED storm delivers, wind and noise and rain,
Monsoons are here, the GREAT BIG WET attacks the coast again.
The lightning CRACKLES, the thunder ROARS and branches start to break,
An endless devastating force, when will this STORM abate?
The tree in which their hollow lives, now dead for many years,
With no more strength, begins to yield, its OCKY's greatest fear.
A sudden CRACK, the tree is split; the storm comes raging through,
It picks him up and flings him out, there's nothing he can do.
He tumbles here and flutters there; he beats his wings so hard,
But the storm it has no mercy, it shows him no regard.
He's carried on for hours and hours, or at least that's how it seems,
More terrifying and fearful than the worst of all his dreams.
When just as fast as it began, the wind and rain all cease,
He spreads his wings, enjoys the breeze and momentary peace.
Then suddenly it dawns on him, he never learned to FLY,
He spirals ever downward, to the ground all scorched and dry.
A mighty THUD, he sees some stars and then the darkness falls,
Only to be woken by a thing with spines and claws.

TOO LONG BEFORE SOMETHING HAPPENS

'Gidday" it says, 'and who are you and where did you come from?'
'I saw you fall from way up there, from high above the SUN!'
'My name is OCKY and I am scared, I'm lost and all alone.
The storm came through and picked me up and took me far from home.'
'You're not alone, just look around, there are many friends right here,
I'm Eddie the Echidna', he said with friendly cheer.
'The dingo's Doug, there's Bilby Bill and well Claire's a crocodile',
And not to mention Rosie Roo and Cookie's laughing smile'.
'There's Eric emu and Fred the frilly, but Carla well she's unique,
A koala in her gumtree she'll just eat the leaves and sleep.'
'We'll play a game, let's call in Pat - flat tail, webbed feet and bill,
And don't forget our Tassie beast; Ted's really got some skill.'
'Hey gather round come meet my friend who's come from far away,
This here is OCKY and he is beaut, let's help him find his way.'
'But first let's play and have some fun, there's time for all the rest,
And have some food, a little nap and then we'll find your nest.'
They ran between the ant hills and jumped with childish ease,
They even got old Carla to come down from behind her leaves.
Played hide and seek and peekaboos and swam in the billabong,
And after lunch on shaded grass, took turns to sing a song.
Then all his friends, they gathered round, the tall, the short, the stout,
And said 'let's go and find your home, it is time for walkabout'.

NO REAL PLOT

CRITICAL ISSUES:
① **MAIN CHARACTER DOESN'T SOLVE PROBLEM!**
② **NO REAL PLOT/STORY**
③ **STORM TAKES UP 35% OF STORY**

520 WORDS

Compared to the rewrite I did this year. The action happens faster, there is an obvious story line, the rhyming scheme is corrected, and the main character solves the problem. I removed almost 160 words, and made the story stronger. It is now 361 words.

INTRODUCE CHARACTER EARLY — Deep inside a hollow tree, all warm and safe in his home. / Lives a red tailed cockatoo, who's frightened and alone. — *PROBLEM / THEME*

Outside a fearsome storm delivers, driving winds and rain, / The GREAT BIG WET, or hurricane attacks the coast again.

OBSTACLE #1 — A sudden crack, the tree is split; the storm comes raging through, / It picks him up and flings him out, there's nothing he can do.

When just as fast as it began, the wind and rain all cease, / He spreads his wings, enjoys the breeze and momentary peace.

Then suddenly it dawns on him. He never learned to fly. — *OBSTACLE #2* / He spirals ever downward, to the ground all scorched and dry.

A mighty thud, he sees some stars and then the darkness falls. / When he's gently woken by something with spines and claws.

'Gidday,' he said, 'are you OK that didn't look like fun?' / 'I saw you fall from way up there, from high above the sun!'

'I'm Ocky, and I'm terrified. I'm lost and all alone.' — *OBSTACLE #3* / 'There was a storm that smashed my tree and took me far from home.'

'I'm Eric the Echidna', he said with friendly cheer. / 'You're not alone. Look about, we're all lost critters here,' — *ALL CREATURES HAVE SAME PROBLEM [LOST!]*

RULE OF 3's —
'The dingo's Doug, there's Bilby Bill and well Claire's a crocodile,' / 'Let's not forget sweet Rosie Roo and Cookie's laughing smile.'
'Meet Emu Ed and Frilly Fred, and Carla, she's unique,' / 'A koala in her gumtree she eats the leaves to sleep.'
'Let's play a game, we'll call in Pat - flat tail, webbed feet and bill,' / 'And don't forget our Tassie beast; Ted's really got some skill.'

'Hey gather round and meet my friend he's come from far away,' / 'Say hi to OCKY, he's a beaut, let's show him how we play.'

INTERLUDE — So they ran between the ant hills and jumped with childish ease. / Ocky even got Carla to forget about her trees.

Played hide and seek and inland games and swam the billabong. / Then after lunch on shaded grass, took turns to sing a song.

IN CHARACTER SOLVES PROBLEM - LIMPT — Then Ocky called to his new friends. The tall, the short, the stout. / 'We need to find our way back home. Come join my walkabout.' — *RESOLUTION*

361 WORDS

2ND DRAFT 3RD DRAFT 4TH DRAFT...

OK! Let's go back to our story the Tadpole That Ate Too Much!

1. One warm summer's night, by the light of the moon, a lonely egg lay on the surface of a pond.
2. In the morning, as the sun warmed the water, the egg hatched and out popped...
3. A Teeny Weeny Tadpole.
4. Frightened and alone, her tummy grumbled. She was starving, so she swam around, looking for something to eat.
5. She was so Teeny Weeny, what could she eat?
6. On Monday morning she saw 1 piece of algae float by 'CHOMP!' It tasted horrible! But she was starving, so she gobbled it up. Then, to her surprise, she grew a leg.
7. On Tuesday morning she saw 2 small leaves, 'CHOMP! MUNCH!' They were tough to swallow. She was still starving when, without warning, she grew another leg.
8. On Wednesday morning she saw something different in the water, 3 squiggly, wriggly mosquito larvae, 'CHOMP! MUNCH! GULP!' They were tasty and super squishy, but she was still starving. To make matters worse, she grew a third leg.
9. On Thursday morning she found 4 water striders. They were fast, but her muscular legs made her faster and 'CHOMP! MUNCH, GULP! CRUNCH!' They were super crunchy, but she was still starving, and she grew a fourth leg.
10. On Friday morning, 5 fat dragonflies landed on the water. 'CHOMP! MUNCH, GULP! CRUNCH! SQUISH!' They were delicious, but she was still starving, and now she had this huge sticky tongue that wouldn't stay in her mouth.
11. On Saturday morning with her long, sticky tongue she ate 1 long leech, 1 slow shrimp, 1 wriggling worm, 1 fat fly, 1 cranky caterpillar, 1 scary spider, 1 brittle beetle, 1 giant grasshopper, 1 tiny turtle, and 1 mighty mouse.
12. Finally, she was no longer starving. She had eaten so much that now her tummy hurt!
13. So she lay on a lily pad and drifted off to sleep, then without warning... 'PLOP!' Her tail fall off!
14. On Sunday, as the rays of the sun warmed the surface of the pond, she realised she was no longer a teeny weeny tadpole. She had four muscular legs and a long, sticky tongue. She was a big, beautiful ~~FROG~~. TOAD! Ewwwww!
15. One warm summer's night, by the light of the moon, a Big Beautiful TOAD lay seven eggs on the surface of a pond.

ADD THE ZING!

As you can see, the revision stage can go on and on.... Let's review my 4th revision and what ELEMENTS I added to make it more engaging for the kids.

I looked for areas in the story that I could add ONOMATOPOEIA or sound effect words

On Monday morning, she saw 1 piece of algae float by 'CHOMP!' It tasted horrible!

If you remember another element of storytelling that always engages the reader is REPETITION so I combined the sounded words with an element of repetition.

CHOMP!
CHOMP! MUNCH!
CHOMP! MUNCH! GULP!
CHOMP! MUNCH! GULP! CRUNCH!
CHOMP! MUNCH! GULP! CRUNCH! SQUISH!

The reader has to repeat the previous sound effects and add a new one each time the tadpole eats something. It is a simple thing to add to the story, but makes it even more enjoyable for those kids just learning to read.

Another tool in the bag of tricks was ALLITERATION, if you remember words starting with the same sound (and often letter). So when the flow of the story changed, I added a section of alliteration to keep the story bouncy and fun.

WRIGGLING WORM,
FAT FLY, CRANKY CATERPILLAR,
SCARY SPIDER, BRITTLE BEETLE, GIANT GRASSHOPPER,
TINY TURTLE, AND MIGHTY MOUSE.

Time to go over your manuscript and look for areas you can add

THE RULE OF 3's, REPETITION
ALLITERATION, ASSONANCE, AND
ONOMATOPOEIA.

12. STEPS TO EDITING

Congratulations! You now have a picture book manuscript completed, and you are probably super excited. It is an impressive achievement and one you should be really proud of, but before you head of to the traditional or self-publishing options, it needs to be edited.

I *HIGHLY* recommend sending your manuscript off to a professional editor before sending to a publisher or agent. It costs a bit of money, but most editors charge by the word count, and given we are talking about picture books of around 500 words, it's not that expensive.

Editors I have used include:

> **WILDFLOWER BOOKS**
> *https://www.wildflowerbooks.net/*

and

> **MARINA CATHERINE EDITING SERVICES**
> *https://www.marinacatherine.com.au/editing-services*

But there are some steps you can take even before sending it off to an editor to help tighten up your manuscript. The first step is *PROOF READING* your story.

We've all done it before, reading over your document to make sure all the words you meant to be there are, and that you correct any obvious spelling mistakes. Now another thing to look for is the basic formatting of your document. When you do your research on which publisher you want to send your story to, you would have checked their publishing guidelines. Most publishers ask for 12 pt Times New Roman with double-spaced paragraphs. So double check the guidelines and then check the complete document to make sure it is exactly what they specify.

The most effective way to proofread a document is to print it out so that you can read it. Reading from a computer screen doesn't have the same effect (well, at least that is my experience). If you print it out, you can have a pen or pencil handy and correct or highlight anything that doesn't seem correct.

Read your words aloud. There are two reasons for this. First, reading aloud forces the brain to slow down. We have a habit of mentally putting in words that are missing if we read in our heads, but reading aloud forces us to read every word and highlights those that are missing.

Second, if you are writing in rhyme, having someone else read it aloud will let you know if the rhythm or beats are in the right spots, and if your rhyming scheme is working. If you can't get someone to read it for you, record yourself reading it and then listen to it.

Once you have completed those steps, final proof reading is to check your regular spelling and grammar mistakes. Everyone has those couple of words they mess up all the time. You might put the 'E' and the 'I' around the wrong way in words like RECEIVE or you might spell 'PRINCIPAL' instead of 'PRINCIPLE', simple minor mistakes.

And the grammar mistakes such as 'RUN-ON SENTENCES', or 'COMMA SPLICING'. A run-on sentence is where you join two independent clauses without punctuation or correct conjunction (and, but, if). A comma splice is very similar. It uses a comma to join to clauses with no appropriate conjunction.

Here's an example:

> Matt B is very clever, he began drawing when he was three years old.

To fix this, remove the comma splice, put in a full stop and capitalise the next word

> Matt B is very clever. He began drawing when he was three years old.

After Proof reading comes the *LINE EDIT*. Line editing is where you review your manuscript line by line (as the name implies). You look for consistency, creativity and conciseness. Especially in picture books where words are at a premium, reviewing the words you have used to ensure you *SHOW* and don't *TELL*, remove any unnecessary adjectives or weak adverbs. Where possible, remove any cliché's unless they are pivotal to your story. Focus on the action. Is there a '*DOING*' activity in each sentence?

The final Edit that you can perform before sending to an Editor is the *STRUCTURAL EDIT* also known as a developmental edit. The principal focus of a Structural Edit is on:

PACING: are there any places in the story that lag or slow down?
CHARACTER DEVELOPMENT: are the characters rounded and real?
PLOT: is it plausible? Are there gaps in the plot?
STORY STRUCTURE: does the story have a start, middle, and end?
WRITING STYLE: Does language and style suit genre and age?
VOICE/TENSE: ARE THEY CONSISTENT THROUGHOUT THE STORY?
SETTING: is there enough world building to make it believable?

Pretty much everything we discussed when initially creating the story. Here are some checklists to help with your editing process.

PROOF-READING CHECKLIST

- [ ] Format your work as Times New Roman 12pt, double spaced and print it out.

- [ ] Read your work out loud. If possible, have someone else read it back to you.

- [ ] Check your work for mistakes that you normally make.

- [ ] Check your grammar and spelling using Grammarly or Pro writing app.

Line Edit Checklist

Show – Don't Tell – have you used the active voice instead of the passive voice? ☐

Check your metaphors or similes do they add value to your story? ☐

Have you removed any unnecessary adverbs and adjectives? ☐

Have you removed any unnecessary clichés? ☐

Did you check your work for mistakes in spelling and grammar? ☐

Did you use the active voice wherever possible? ☐

Did you simplify your writing using the Pro Writing App or another tool? ☐

STRUCTURAL EDIT CHECKLIST

Does your introduction invoke curiosity in the reader? ☐

Does the action/problem start early in your story? ☐

Do you use one of the five senses in each page? ☐

Did you tell a story? ☐

Are there visual elements in your writing? ☐

What's the weakest part of your work? Now, can you cut it? ☐

Are the stanzas of a consistent length? ☐

Is the tone of voice appropriate? ☐

13. MANUSCRIPT ASSESSMENT

I have added a chapter on Manuscript Assessments as they follow on from having your manuscript edited. A manuscript assessment takes a manuscript that is ready to submit to a publisher and breaks it down into crucial segments to test the viability of the story for commercial publication.

Now this can be a little daunting the first few times you do it, but believe me, it is well worth the expense, and personal pain in having your story looked at critically by experienced editors and publishers.

So what do they look for in your manuscript that differs from a standard edit?

In a manuscript assessment they will still check for grammar, spelling and story structure, however they go to the next level and provide comments on where you are strong and what is weak. Sometimes the feedback can feel harsh, but it is always constructive and comes from a place of helping you to create a stronger, more engaging story.

Once you have had a few assessments done, you will automatically think about the critical elements, even when you are writing your next story. It will make you a stronger writer and more likely to be picked up by a publisher or agent.

One thing I would like to highlight here is that often a publishing house will offer manuscript assessments as part of their services. If you have a great story that is well edited, it is a great way to bypass the submission process (especially for those who do not accept manuscripts from authors without an agent) as once they do a manuscript assessment, if they like the story they will open discussions with you about taking the next steps.

So let's have a look at a manuscript assessment template.

| SECTION | TEMPLATE | NOTES |

PLOT:
Is there a beginning, middle and end, or is the plot cyclical?
Are conflict and resolution present?
Does the plot build or lag?
Does the story have an interesting resolution/ending?

STORY STRUCTURE:
Does the story flow well and pull the reader along with it?
Does the text hold reader attention?

TEXT:
Is the text creatively written and does it flow well? Or will the reader stumble over its construction?
Is the text too wordy, slowing the pace and creating confusion?
Does the text show, not tell?

CHARACTERS:
Is the work creative and inspiring?
Is it clever, funny, and fascinating?
Is the work 'different' and original?
Does it challenge the reader and advance the genre?

CREATIVITY & ORIGINALITY:
Is the work creative and inspiring?
Is it clever, funny, and fascinating?
Is the work 'different' and original?
Does it challenge the reader and advance the genre?

SUITABILITY:
Is the subject matter age-appropriate?
Would it draw in children?
Is it moralistic or patronising?

GRAMMAR & PUNCTUATION:
Does the author need to work on their grammar, punctuation and presentation, or is it spot-on?

Part Five
****

Draw On The Artist Within

14. THE ILLUSTRATIONS

By this stage, you have a magnificent manuscript that you are proud to send to a publisher. But what about the pictures? This is a *PICTURE BOOK* after all.

There are two options to investigate.
OPTION 1: Illustrate your own story,
OPTION 2: Look to outsource this to another illustrator?
If you are looking to get a traditional publisher, you normally do not need to worry about finding an illustrator, as each publishing house has a stable of illustrators they use. It is still valuable for Authors to understand the illustration process or vision for the artwork so that they can provide illustrator notes or discuss your vision with the artist.

Let's look at some general illustration terminology that you will need to be familiar with.

SPOT ILLUSTRATION: A spot illustration is a small, well defined, floating illustration often with no background.

VIGNETTE: A vignette is a small illustration with faded edges. It incorporates the white of the background to achieve a loose look.

HALF PAGE: A half page indicates that approximately half the page contains the illustration. The illustration can be on the top, bottom or even either side, leaving half the page white for the text to sit.

FULL PAGE: A full page is exactly as it sounds the illustration covers the entire page, it can have a section of white space for the text to be located or it can be completely coloured.

DOUBLE SPREAD: A double spread is one continuous illustration that covers two consecutive pages. The text can occur either on one or both pages.

Then Eric called out to his friends,   The tall, the short, the stout

BLUE PAGE: A blue page is a page with no text at all. It is normally a double spread that occurs close to the middle of the story or where the pace of the story needs to change.

OK, so now we know all the important terminology for picture book illustrations let's move onto what to do next. To the writer who wants to self-publish but doesn't want to illustrate the book themselves, you will need to find an illustrator and negotiate an illustrator agreement with them. (I have a sample agreement in the resources section).

FIND AN ILLUSTRATOR

One of the most challenging tasks for a picture book author is finding an illustrator who will bring their story to life. There are a million people online purporting to be picture book artists, and a lot even use other people's artwork and try to pass it off as their own. So how do you avoid these dodgy flim-flammers? There is an age-old adage that says:

YOU GET WHAT YOU PAY FOR!

And this still holds true today. While there are a lot of emerging artists wanting to break into the industry who will undervalue their artwork just to get the project, the rule of thumb is if you pay for quality, you get quality. Now if you are an emerging artist wanting to break into illustrating picture books, keep this truism in mind.

PRICE YOUR WORK APPROPRIATELY

Don't chase a project at the expense of your art form. Build your KIDSLIT portfolio and put it out there and you will get the work.

OK, so where do you find legitimate, trustworthy illustrators? There are two places you can start your search. The first one is The Society of Children's Book Writers and Illustrators - known as:

SCBWI
HTTPS://WWW.SCBWI.ORG

The second great source for quality, reputable and professional illustrators is the Australian Society Of Authors - Style File.

THE STYLE FILE
HTTPS://.ASASTYLEFILE.COM

You can also search for picture book illustrators on the internet and there are many Facebook groups dedicated to the KidsLit genre. Some popular *FaceBook Groups* are:

KidsLit Writers and Illustrators
HTTPS://WWW.FACEBOOK.COM/GROUPS/492668911435207

Children's Book Writers and Illustrators
HTTPS://WWW.FACEBOOK.COM/GROUPS/1873504253469715/

Just Write for Kids Australia
HTTPS://WWW.FACEBOOK.COM/GROUPS/JUSTWRITEFORKIDS

Creative Kids Tales Network
HTTPS://WWW.FACEBOOK.COM/GROUPS/CREATIVEKIDSTALESNETWORK/

Children's Writer's & Illustrator's Market
HTTPS://WWW.FACEBOOK.COM/GROUPS/ILLUSTRATORSANDWRITERS/

Children's Book Illustrators
HTTPS://WWW.FACEBOOK.COM/GROUPS/3240620214

Children's Book Author Community
HTTPS://WWW.FACEBOOK.COM/GROUPS/953747601653911

And many more... Just look at the community, engage in the posts and ask questions. You will find the KidsLit community love to support emerging writers and illustrators.

WORKING WITH AN ILLUSTRATOR

OK, so you have done your research, and found the perfect illustrator, what do you do next? There are two crucial documents you should have ready before approaching an illustrator with your manuscript.

The first one is an **NDA** or a **NON-DISCLOSURE AGREEMENT**. A non-disclosure agreement is used to protect your manuscript when sending it to illustrators or other interested parties. Imagine this: you have taken a year to write, edit and polish your story, and then you send it to an illustrator to get a quote on them illustrating your story. The unscrupulous illustrator thinks, hey this is an awesome story. I'm going to steal the idea (or even plagiarise the entire thing) and illustrates and publishes it. You are heartbroken, and while there are legal options to pursue, it can become very complex, time-consuming and expensive.

So avoiding this scenario, before you send any story off, send the interested party an **NDA**, which stipulates who the **CONTRACTOR** (or illustrator) is, who the **CLIENT** (or author) is and that all information is confidential and belongs to the client bla bla blaaa...

After the NDA comes the **ILLUSTRATOR AGREEMENT** or **CONTRACT**. This is the documentation that is normally supplied by the illustrator, however, it is important that you are familiar with the elements of the agreement prior to entering negotiations. It doesn't hurt to have your own Illustrator Agreement ready just in case you are working with a very talented illustrator who is new to the industry.

Let's have a look at the major sections you need to know.

IMPORTANT CAVEAT

Always seek professional advice before entering any contract or legal agreement. The documents here are for demonstration only!

PROJECT TITLE ( )

DESCRIPTION :
(Qty) single page digital colour illustrations
(Qty) double spread digital colour illustrations
Cover (wrap around digital colour illustration)

FEE: $

SCHEDULE (due dates)
Rough Sketch: _____, Colours _____,Final : _____.

COPYRIGHT USAGE - Outlines the exact usage allowed, unless you stipulate you want the copyright (at an additional fee) the illustrator retains the copyright on all images.

1) RESERVATION OF RIGHTS: All rights not expressly granted above are retained by the Illustrator,

2) REVISIONS: how many revisions are allowed before extra fee charged and when in the schedule they can occur.

3) CANCELLATION AND KILL FEES: Sometimes the project gets cancelled, this is the section where you negotiate the percentage that is paid out on cancellation or Killing of the project.

4) CREDITS AND COPIES: Whether the Illustrator gets credit on the cover and how many copies of the book they receive as part of this agreement

5) PAYMENT: e.g. 40% deposit on signing, 30% payment on delivery of roughs, final 30% payment for finished work is due upon acceptance, net fourteen (14) days.

6) PERMISSIONS AND RELEASES: outlines the indemnity of parties if they infringe on someone else's copyright.

Signed by the Illustrator ……………………………..
Signed for and on behalf of the Client ……………………………………..

BUT I AM THE ILLUSTRATOR!

That's the boring stuff out of the way. So now onto what's required if you want to illustrate your own story or another author's story?

As a regular speaker at KidsLit Events and schools, one question (or more accurately, the excuse) I get for people not illustrating their own stories is that they are traditional artists and cannot use digital applications. The reality is that some of the best picture book illustrators in the world use traditional mediums. Look at Graeme Base or Alex Scheffler to name a couple.

In reality, it doesn't matter what style you use as long as the illustrations are **APPEALING, VIVID, ENGAGING** and **FUN**.

In the following sections, we will look at the actual steps I follow when creating picture book illustrations. Let's have a quick overview of the steps and then go into each one in more detail.

- KNOW YOUR PRINT JARGON
- CHOOSE YOUR ART MEDIUM
- BREAK APART THE MANUSCRIPT
- USING THUMBNAILS
- PAGE LAYOUTS
- CREATE CHARACTERS
- USING REFERENCE
- COMPOSITION – RULE OF 3RDS
- COVER ART
- USING INDESIGN

15. PRINT JARGON

Now, I know I said I would write this book with the minimum of fluff and technical jargon, but there are a couple of things you will need to understand when creating your illustrations for a book.

The terms we are going to talk about in this lesson are: Trim Line, Gutter, Page Numbers, Bleed, Safe Zone, DPI, RGB, CMYK and Image File Types.

I promise I will make this brief and painless... OK, so let's start.

TRIM LINE

The *TRIM LINE* is the box that shows you where you can illustrate your pictures. I set the trim line to the exact dimensions of the actual size of the book.

So why do they call it Trim, well that's a good question? When the printers set up your pages, they use sheets of paper stock that are larger than the final physical book and then they cut down or trim them to the correct size. Sometimes the publisher may include the actual dimension in millimetres or inches on the template. The width being first and height being second.

PAGER NUMBERS

PAGE NUMBERS are pretty self-explanatory, but I had to add it. It is also a very important element when you consider your naming conventions for illustrations like TWT_pg6-7.png or when communicating with the client about a specific illustration. Eg: page 6 Illustration.

In most cases, for picture books, when you deliver your file to the publisher/client for printing, you won't be delivering single pages at a time, you will deliver spreads like pg 6-7, pg 8-9 etc. The printer will then print each spread as one page and bind them along the gutter.

GUTTER

The Gutter: The line that cuts one big page (a double spread) in half, making two pages. The gutter falls into the spine of the book; it is very important to remember the fold created by binding the book, which can affect art and text. Don't forget to number each page.

BLEED

The Bleed is the term that confuses most illustrators (including me when I first ventured into illustrating kid's books). Also referred to as the bleed guide or bleed line. Often the printer will accompany it with text instructions showing exactly how much bleed to give in your illustrations. As an example, a 3mm bleed all the way around is common.

So what exactly is *BLEED?* We just discussed how a book, when printed, is larger than the final dimensions and then Trimmed down. A rookie mistake (and one I have made when starting out) would be to do your illustrations only to the trim guide, now when that page gets printed and trimmed to its final size, there is a high probability that there may be alignment issues in printing and trimming resulting in a white line appearing on pages.

While this may look minor to you, it will require the publisher to order a reprint, now imagine if they just printed 10000 copies of the book, these books would have to be trashed, this would be a huge expense in money and time for the publisher and would most likely result in you being fired, or at the very least not getting hired again. Let's avoid that outcome. The solution is to extend your illustrations up to or beyond the bleed line.

An important note here is to only extend background elements, don't have any important information go past the trim line. To avoid this happening, I create guides for myself which I call the *SAFE ZONE.*

SAFE ZONE

The **SAFE ZONE** is a guide I created to ensure the critical elements of my illustrations remain safe during the **TRIM** stage. So how do I determine the measurements needed to ensure a **SAFE ZONE?** I take whatever the **TRIM LINE** dimensions are, say 3mm, and I create a guide with that measurement inside the trim line. This ensures that no matter what happens with the printing and trimming, the essential elements for the visual narrative remain safely on the page.

DPI

DPI, or dots per inch, measures the resolution of a printed document or digital scan. The higher the dot density, the higher the resolution of the print or scan. Typically, *DPI* measures the number of dots that are placed in a line across one inch, or 2.54 centimetres.

The higher the *DPI*, the sharper the image. A higher resolution image provides the printer and printing device more information. You can get more detail and greater resolution from an image with higher *DPI*.

A lower *DPI* will produce an image with fewer dots in printing. No matter how powerful your printer is, a low-resolution image doesn't provide enough raw data to produce high-quality images. The ink will spread on the page, making the edges look fuzzy.

1. Low-Resolution Images: 150dpi and less are considered low resolution. Low-resolution images are blurry and pixelated after printing.

2. Medium-Resolution Images: between 200dpi - 300dpi. The industry standard for quality photographs and image is typically 300dpi.

3. High-Resolution Images: 300dpi - 600dpi is considered to be a high-resolution image or print.

RGB vs CMYK

Your computer monitor or TV displays images using 3 overlapping colours: **RED** (R), **GREEN** (G), and **BLUE** (B). Commonly referred to as *RGB*-format data.

On the other hand, printing machines used for full-colour printing of books use **CYAN** (C), **MAGENTA** (M), **YELLOW** (Y), and a **KEY** (K) plate also known as true **BLACK** inks for printing fine halftone dots this is why it is referred to as *CMYK*. These halftone dots of each colour are then superimposed or overlaid on each other to create the various colours.

FILE TYPES

OK, last bit of jargon I want to discuss is file types. Each publisher or client will have their own guidelines for how they want you to provide the illustrations, so first and foremost, check those guidelines and follow every instruction to the letter.

Generally, there are 5 file types for sending illustrations, the first 3 relate to raster images. Raster images use little blocks or pixels of colour. The preferred format for these are high resolution: JPEG, PNG or TIFF files.

You can use PDF documents for sharing raster illustrations with stakeholders or clients prior to getting the sign off, but it isn't the preferred method for delivering final art work.

The exception here is for vector files. Vector files keep clarity regardless of how much you resize them. Vector files are built using mathematical (beiser) formulas that establish points on a grid and can infinitely adjust in size without losing resolution. The best formats for these are: SVG or PDF.

4. BLEED

3. PAGE NUMBERS

2. GUTTER

1. TRIM LINE

5. SAFE ZONE

extend art to this line (3mm bleed)

important elements stay within trim lines

background elements extend to bleed

16. ART MEDIUMS

A quick word about Art Mediums in KidsLit. Whatever tool you use to create your illustrations is called a medium. Often, artists use more than one medium on each illustration. For example, Graeme Base uses watercolour, pencil and gauche in his traditional illustrations. Even digital artists use multiple digital mediums within one piece, combining digital pencil, watercolour, airbrush, and textures etc.

Traditional Illustrations can include: GRAPHITE PENCIL, COLOUR PENCIL, INK PENS, COPIC MARKERS, WATERCOLOUR, GAUCHE, OILS, AIRBRUSH, INK WASH AND EVEN COFFEE OR TEA.

Pencil Sketch

There are also many digital applications used to create picture book illustrations. They all have their pros and cons.

Here is a list of programmes I have used. COREL PAINTER, CLIP STUDIO, PROCREATE (IPAD), ADOBE PHOTOSHOP, ADOBE ILLUSTRATOR, KRITA (OPEN SOURCE), INKSCAPE (OPEN SOURCE), PAINTSTORM, REBELLE, AUTODESK SKETCHBOOK, AND COREL DRAW.

Digital Pencil

Digital Ink

Whether you prefer to use traditional illustration techniques, digital applications or a combination of both, the choice is yours! Experiment, maybe you will find a combination that is uniquely yours that will help you stand out from the crowd.

17. THE MANUSCRIPT

The first step to illustrating a picture book is taking the manuscript and breaking it apart. When I first started out illustrating books for children, I made the very simple mistake of illustrating exactly what the words described. A lot of emerging illustrators make this mistake, reading through the story only once and then creating the artwork to match the words. Now for the younger reading audience, that is ok, having the pictures mirror the words, but for the most part the job of an illustrator is to enhance the text, add more meaning, and sometimes to illustrate the complete opposite.

My process for breaking the manuscript apart is fairly simple.

STEP 1. I print the manuscript and then read through the complete story with no preconceptions. That's right, just read it.

STEP 2. Read through the story again, this time with a pencil or pen. In the margins I make notes about feelings, thoughts, colours, characters. Sometimes I even make brief thumbnail sketches, but I will go into that in more depth in the next chapter.

STEP 3. Using the left margin note where the story fits into the 3 Act structure. Make notes when the character appears, the conflicts or challenges, the rising tension leading to the climax, and where the story meets a resolution. (See example on page 100)

STEP 4. Sometimes, I print another copy and cut up the stanzas so I can place them on a larger sheet of paper for roughing out pages, double spreads, and page turns. I set nothing in stone and you should change things when it doesn't feel right.

Now, if you are working on someone else's manuscript, there is one rule you cannot break. You *CANNOT* change any of the wording. Even if you feel it will improve the story. You can decide how much of the text sits on any one page, but that is the limit to your artistic license.

So now you have a manuscript, you have read through it several times and made some notes relating to how it makes you feel, how you see the character, and an overall feeling about what the author is trying to convey.

Now there is **ONE** very important step that a lot of illustrators (even those who have illustrated several books) often cannot grasp.

You are illustrating a book for children, young children from between 3 years to 8 years. Put yourself in the mind of a kid. When you read the words on the page, try to envisage what images a child might see.

Kids see simple events as hilariously funny, overwhelmingly dark or simply out of context with what we as adults perceive to be the norm.

One way to connect with kids is in the colour palette you choose. Regardless of your colour theory, **ANALOGOUS**, **COMPLEMENTARY** or **SPLIT COMPLEMENTARY** the colours need to be **VIVID!**

BRIGHT, VIVID colours draw the child into the story. When looking at how you break the manuscript apart, think of how you will use colour to better tell the story. When you read the story, if it talks about a sad topic, think of using cool colours. If the story calls for happy, up beat emotions think of using a warmer colour set, it is ok to change the colours throughout the story.

Most stories will also have a section where the pace or action changes. They often refer to this as a blue page (and no, it doesn't have to be blue) it is a double page spread that often has no words, simply a change in pace or action, followed by the rest of the story.

Try to identify this part of the manuscript and make a note on how you might show the change in the story through colour or use of illustration.

Let's look at an example of how I break down the manuscript for the story.

185 WORDS

INTRODUCE CHARACTER ↴

'Hey there Doug, do you want some sea SNAIL?' ← REGULAR ORCA BEHAVIOUR

'No thanks Gus I'm enjoying some KALE' ← HAPPY WITH HIS HEALTHY CHOICE

OBSTACLE #1
'Stop playing games, let's go eat that BIRD!' ← GUS UPSET!
'Oh I don't eat meat, haven't you heard?' ← DOUG PROUD DOESN'T EAT MEAT

OBSTACLE #2
'Stop it Doug, you know we eat SEALS!' ← GUS GETTING FRUSTRATED
'But I like spuds and peas with my meals' ← DOUG LOOKS CONFUSED

OBSTACLE #3
'Are you crazy! Now go eat that TURTLE!'
'I'd much rather eat these berries of myrtle.'
← ORCA'S GET ANGRY / ANIMALS HAPPY BEING DOUG

OBSTACLE #4
'You've got to be joking now come eat this SHARK!'
'But I've just baked my famous fruit tart!'

OBSTACLE #5
'For the sake of all Orcas, help eat this SQUID!'
'Try some KELP it's divine, I can't tell a Fib.'
← MAYBE HAVE EPIC BATTLE WITH SQUID WINNING

OBSTACLE #6
'You're just being silly, let's go eat those FISH!' ← GUS GETTING ANGRY
'Three Fruit, five Veg, what a colourful dish.' ← MAKE COLOURFUL HIGHLIGHT FRUIT/VEG

RISING TENSION
⎡ 'DOUG! You can't eat cabbage
  Potatoes or greens! You can't eat fruits   ← MAYBE TEXT ONLY
  Legumes or beans, You can't eat truffles   WORD ART
  You can't eat KALE!'   NO ILLUSTRATIONS
  'Look in the mirror, you're a KILLER WHALE!' ← BE FUNNY TO HAVE GUS HOLDING UP A MIRROR
  'Ok then, I will say no more...
⎣

INTERLUDE
But only if you try my COLESLAW!' ← DOUG HAPPY
'OK...' ← BLUE PAGE ORCAS EATING NO TEXT
'So what is the verdict, Did I serve up a treat?'
'It sure was tasty...But... we still prefer...'

CLIMAX 'MEAT!' → ORCAS LOOK HUNGRY DOUG CONFUSED ANIMALS RUN AWAY

RESOLUTION...

ADD STEM PAGE

YOUR TURN

OK, it's your turn. Have a go at breaking a manuscript apart. Remember the basic steps, there is no right or wrong answer... Below is one of my stories... Break it apart.

MY FAVOURITE THING! © Matt B Lewis 2021
I woke up today and wondered, what's BEST?

What's the one thing I love more than the rest?

My BATS and BALLS or my library of BOOKS.

BLOCKS I can stack, or my army CHINOOKS.

My toys that can TALK, or rockets that ZOOM

The ALPHABET blocks spread over my room.

Fuzzy the BEAR or robots that BATTLE.

My TAMBORINE or old baby RATTLE.

There's my toy that GIGGLES, or set of DRUMS?

And POSTERS with NUMBERS to learn my SUMS?

WHISTLES, KEYBOARDS or some dusty old FLUTES.

Monster TRUCKS, PLANES, or my TRAIN set that TOOTS.

Pedal-power CAR and TRIKE with paint peeling.

Or LAMP that puts STARS up on my ceiling.

No, my FAVOURITE thing, the one I LOVE MOST!

Is a HUG from mum, and VEGEMITE TOAST!

THE 1ST READ

In the first read, remember to not over think the story, when you read it what is the first thoughts or images that come to mind? Write some thoughts here:

THE 2ND READ

In the second read, is all about the emotion, what do you feel, what are your thoughts on the character (human, animal, other). Write your notes here:

THE 3RD READ

In the next read, think about where you see the story fit in relation to the 3 Act Structure, how will you introduce your character. Which part of the story is the interlude or climax? Write notes here:

NOTES

Use this page to make notes on the story. Remember to think about how kids view the world.

HOW I WORKED THE MANUSCRIPT

MY FAVOURITE THING!   © Matt B Lewis 2021   — MEET EDDIE the ECHIDNA SITTING IN A MESSY ROOM TOYS EVERYWHERE

I woke up today and wondered, what's BEST?

What's the one thing I love more than the rest?   — CLOSE UP OF CORNER ROOM SPECIAL TOYS + A BOOKS HELF. EDDIE HAND ON CHIN?

My BATS and BALLS or my library of BOOKS.   — SEE TOYS + BOOKS — ants IN BG MOVING A BALL... EDDIE HOLDING FAVORITE BOOK

BLOCKS I can stack, or my army CHINOOKS.   — SEE THE ITEMS... ANTS LOADING HELICOPTER UP

My toys that can TALK, or rockets that ZOOM   — ANTS SITTING ON ROCKET AS OTHERS CARRY IT OFF SHOT

The ALPHABET blocks spread over my room.   — ANTS MOVING BLOCKS TO SPELL OUT 'WAR'

Fuzzy the BEAR or robots that BATTLE.   — EDDIE HOLDING BEAR TIGH. ANTS INSIDE BATTLE BOTS...

My TAMBORINE or old baby RATTLE.   — ANTS JUMPING OFF BUSTED BOT, BOUNCING OFF TAMBORINE... RATTLE IN BG

There's my toy that GIGGLES, or set of DRUMS?   — EDDIE PLAYING DRUMS... ANTS BEING BOUNCED + POUNDED

And POSTERS with NUMBERS to learn my SUMS?   — EDDIE LOOKING @ NUMBER CHART ANTS TRY TO BLEND IN + LOOK LIKE NUMBERS

WHISTLES, KEYBOARDS or some dusty old FLUTES.   — EDDIE BLOWS FLUTE... ANTS FLY OUT THE END

Monster TRUCKS, PLANES, or my TRAIN set that TOOTS.   — EPIC ILLO... ANTS IN EVERY MODE OF TRANSPORT

Pedal-power CAR and TRIKE with paint peeling.   — 3 VIGNETTES... EDDIE REMEMBERS RIDING EACH ONE

Or LAMP that puts STARS up on my ceiling.   — EDDIE ASLEEP... LAMP SHINES STARS. SHADOWS OF ANTS UNDERNEATH.

No, my FAVOURITE thing, the one I LOVE MOST!   — EDDIE HOLDING PHOTO OF HIS MUM

(Is a HUG from mum,) and VEGEMITE TOAST!   — CHEEKY EDDIE EATING VEGEMITE TOAST... HUGE SMILE.
↑ MOVE UP TO LINE ABOVE

FORTRESS OF TOYS IN BG WITH ANTS READY FOR BATTLE

130 WORDS

18. THUMBNAILING

Congratulations, you have worked through your manuscript and decided on the emotions, character, and colours the story evokes. You should now have a good understanding of the direction you feel the story is taking.

The next stage in my process is to take the ideas, notes and manuscript and create quick thumbnails to work through my initial ideas. So what is a thumbnail and why do I use them. As human beings, we have a tendency to seek perfection in everything we do, and no one more so than the creative types, like illustrators and authors. Often, this results in us getting in our own way.

We focus on a single illustration or a single component of that illustration trying to get it perfect, and we end up spending so much time on one element that we block the creativity and flow that we need to get the story pacing correct and work out the general compositions.

This led to the art of thumbnailing, allowing artists to quickly work out ideas in small rough drawings. And when I say rough, that is exactly what I mean. They don't have to be anatomically correct, or detailed. They don't even have to be complete characters. Rough, gestural drawings, showing action, movement, placement and or composition.

Why do we spend time on thumbnailing? The simple fact is *SPEED* and *CREATIVITY*. You can smash out 10 to 20 thumbnails in the time it would normally take to do one standard concept illustration. By quickly thumbnailing the story, you can immediately see if something is going to work or not, and make changes without investing a lot of time. If you had created one larger concept illustration, you would be faced with either starting it over from scratch or investing time in trying to fix the compositional issues.

Let's look at how I go about thumbnailing a story.

THE TADPOLE THAT ATE TOO MUCH!

One warm summer's night, by the light of the moon, a lonely egg lay on the surface of a pond. *— ESTABLISH THE WORLD... A POND*

In the morning, as the sun warmed the water, the egg hatched and out popped... *INTRODUCE CHARACTER*
A Teeny Weeny Tadpole.

Frightened and alone, her tummy grumbled. She was starving, so she swam around, looking for something to eat. *THE PROBLEM EMOTION*

She was so Teeny Weeny, what could she eat? *← OBSTACLE #1 ... TINY TADPOLE IN HUGE POND*

On Monday morning she saw 1 piece of algae float by 'CHOMP!' It tasted horrible! But she was starving, so she gobbled it up. Then, to her surprise, she grew a leg. *CONFUSED*

On Tuesday morning she saw 2 small leaves, 'CHOMP! MUNCH!' They were tough to swallow. She was still starving when, without warning, she grew another leg. *ILLUSTRATE REPETITION*

On Wednesday morning she saw something different in the water, 3 squiggly, wriggly mosquito larvae, 'CHOMP! MUNCH! GULP!' They were tasty and super squishy, but she was still starving. To make matters worse, she grew a third leg. *GROWING BIGGER @ EACH STAGE*

On Thursday morning she found 4 water striders. They were fast, but her muscular legs made her faster and 'CHOMP! MUNCH, GULP! CRUNCH!' They were super crunchy, but she was still starving, and she grew a fourth leg. *NEED TO HAVE ADDED THREAT!*

On Friday morning, 5 fat dragonflies landed on the water. 'CHOMP! MUNCH, GULP! CRUNCH! SQUISH!' They were delicious, but she was still starving, and now she had this huge sticky tongue that wouldn't stay in her mouth. *EAGRET/CRANE*

On Saturday morning with her long, sticky tongue she ate 1 long leech, 1 slow shrimp, 1 wriggling worm, 1 fat fly, 1 cranky caterpillar, 1 scary spider, 1 brittle beetle, 1 giant grasshopper, 1 tiny turtle, and 1 mighty mouse. *BLUE PAGE NO POND JUST ANIMALS*

Finally, she was no longer starving. She had eaten so much that now her tummy hurt! So she lay on a lily pad and drifted off to sleep, then without warning... 'PLOP!' her tail fall off! *CHANGE PACE*

On Sunday, as the rays of the sun warmed the surface of the pond, she realised she was no longer a teeny weeny tadpole. She had four muscular legs and a long, sticky tongue. She was a big, beautiful ~~FROG~~. TOAD! Ribbbetttt! *VIGNETS OF EACH ILLO*

One warm summer's night, by the light of the moon, a Big Beautiful TOAD lay seven eggs on the surface of a pond. *← BACK TO START OF STORY*

CRANE FLYS OFF! CAN'T EAT A TOAD

ADD STEM SHEET ON FROGS/TOADS

19. THE STORYBOARD

Once you have your clean thumbnails worked out and you are happy that your overall composition tells the visual story, it is time to create a storyboard.

Storyboards like thumbnails can be rough, or detailed, grey scale or fully coloured and rendered illustrations depending on who you show them to. For Picture Books, a clean grey scale storyboard is usually all you need to present to a literary agent or publisher. Sometimes they may ask to see one or two completed colour versions to make sure it aligns to their vision, but more often than not just the storyboard will suffice.

A storyboard takes the thumbnails to the next level, by cleaning up the elements that work and placing them in the sequence you feel best tells the story it helps to show the rhythm and pacing of the story. There have been times where I was certain of the text and image I wanted on each page of the book right up to story boarding it out. Only to realise it was missing a vital page turn. If I had simply illustrated every page without this revelation it would have resulted in a ton of re-work, lost productivity or worse, a book that didn't resonate with the target readers. This actually happened in my book 'The Tadpole That Ate Too Much!' I had the story thumbnailed and paced out and everything looked good until I noticed a huge mistake.

Take a look at the storyboard on the next page. The spread where the froglet's tail disappears is technically and graphically wrong. I had thumbnailed it falling off and carried it over to the storyboard, but in fact the tail gets absorbed into the body. This was a colossal error and would have made the story lose all credibility. I know what you are thinking, but you put so much time into drawing it, and yes I did render this in colour as a sample to send the publisher, but looking at the storyboard holistically allowed me to pick up on the mistake before it was sent out to a wider audience. I strongly recommend getting into the habit of:

STORYBOARDING

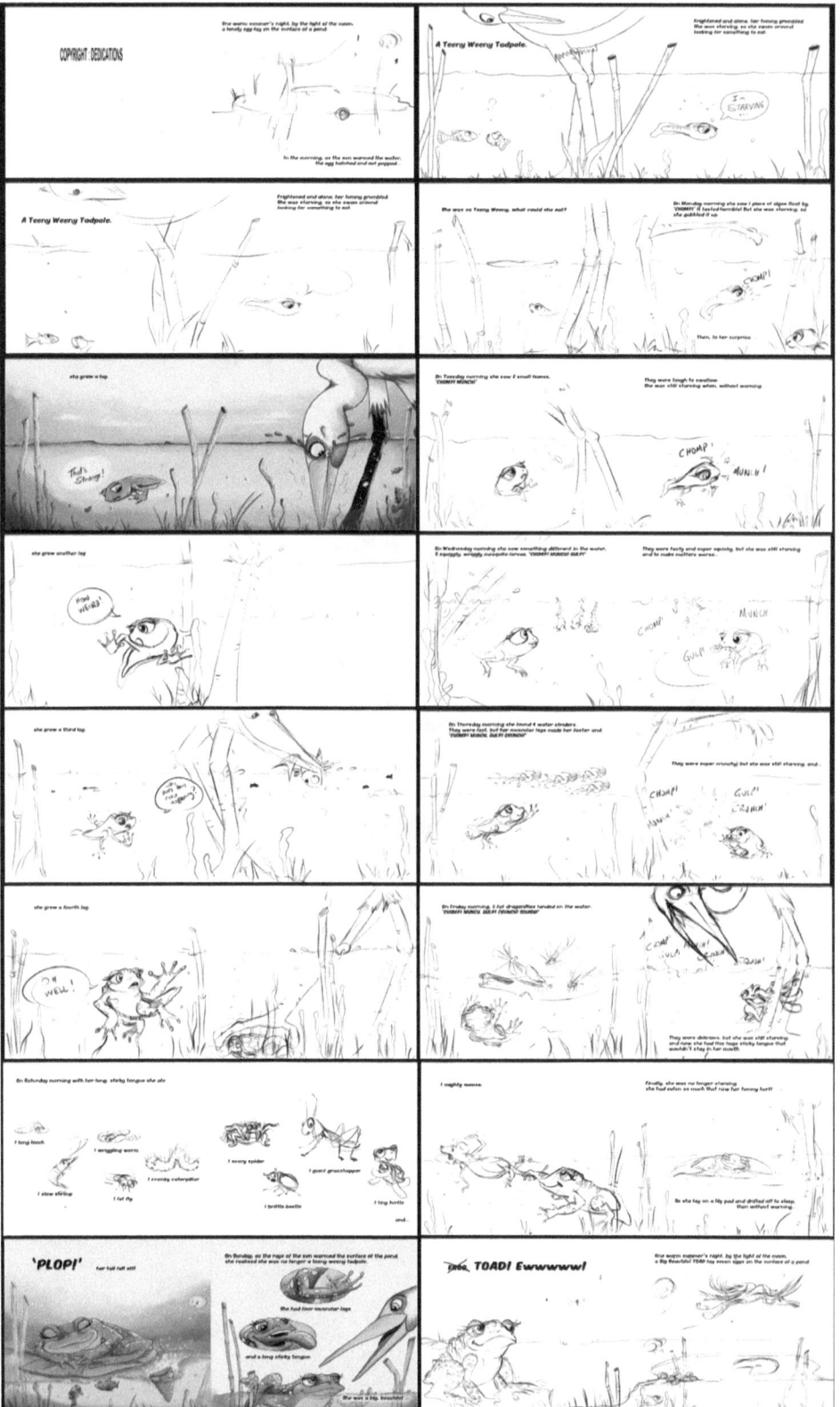

Part Six
✱✱✱✱✱✱✱✱✱✱✱

The Character Is The Action!

20. CHARACTER CREATION 2.0

Ok, so I know exactly what you are thinking, "Hey we already discussed character creation in chapter 4, what gives?

In chapter 4, we looked at creating believable characters that were real. They had physical and character traits we could recognise, as well as flaws, just like actual people. They weren't perfect.

As an illustrator, you now have to imbue these characteristics into a visually engaging character. There are many aspects of character creation from a visual perspective that need to be considered.

Foremost, your character needs to resonate with the target reader. You want the child to empathise with the main character, even if they have bad character flaws. You want them to like your character and root for them to succeed.

One of my all-time favourite examples of this is Gru from Universal Film's Despicable Me franchise.

When you first meet Gru he has all the character traits of the bad guy, he has angular, pointy features, no hair, evil smirk, a scary pet (that resembles a dog) and he drives a monstrosity of a car that puts out more pollution than a small city.

All good reasons to dislike him, and yet there is something about him that everyone loves. He can't help being bad, that's how his mother raised him. Enter the 3 girls, even though he initially hoped to only use them to gain entry into his nemesis, but there is an instant bond, and his character becomes more loving and gentle. Even though he keeps the angular, pointy features.

OK! I digress, but you get the example. How we physically represent our main character is very important when carrying the story.

So what things do you need to consider when creating characters, especially as they relate to kids' Picture Books?

THE 1ST RULE:

AGE: I discussed the first rule of character design in chapter 4, but let's revisit it now. The AGE of the character needs to be within 1 or 2 years of the target reader.

So if you aim your Picture Book at 5-7-year-olds, then your character would be 5 - 9 years old. It is better to make them older rather than younger because most children like to think of themselves being able to do thing older kids can do.

THE 2ND RULE:

CUTENESS: In most cases, kids respond best to cuteness. Even if the character has flaws or bad characteristics, they can still have a certain cuteness to them. Two tricks illustrators use to give their characters this cute factor are:

Head size to body proportion. Young animals and children (and I guess aliens or monsters) have a head that is disproportionately larger than the rest of their body. Think of their head, the top 2/3rds contain a huge brain that they then have to grow into, the bottom 3rd is for the facial features.

THE 3RD RULE:

PUSH THE ACTION: Often, an emerging illustrator will draw a simple character in an almost static pose. For the most part this is **BORING.**

It is perfectly ok to draw static poses for your characters when creating the turnaround (front view, side view and 3/4 view). But once you are happy with your design, you need to push the line of action! Kids love to see the hero **DOING** something. So practice your **GESTURE** drawing, using **FORCE**, and **LINE OF ACTION** to bring your hero to life on the page.

YOUR TURN!

In the first box rough out your character's major design, try to get a front view, side view and a 3/4 view. These don't need to be polished illustrations, just pencil sketches to show consistency of the character. Think of features like clothing or accessories as they may impact the second set of drawings. Once you are happy with the design, move on to putting your character in various action poses.

Turn Around

Action Poses

21. USING REFERENCE

There is a long running debate between people in relation to the use of reference in creating art. Whether you are creating a visual narrative for picture books or a fine art piece for a museum, the process is the same.

Reference is the Secret Tool of the masters like Leonardo da Vinci, Michaelangelo, Vincent van Gogh and all the other amazing artist people pay a squillion dollars to own.

So why the debate? To put it as plainly as possible, there is a HUGE difference between using an image or photo for reference, and using it to trace over. When you start out learning to draw, it is ok to trace when learning how to make the shapes and lines. But once you are creating art for distribution, you shouldn't trace.

Think of your reference like you were attending a life drawing class. The model sets up, strikes a pose, and then you draw what you see. You can't go up to them and put your paper on them to trace their outline.

So why is it important to use reference? Creating illustrations that have a solid foundation based on something real makes your drawings more believable. Especially for kids, remember they see the world as it relates to them. So even if you are creating a fantasy world, or weird creatures, monsters or aliens, having reference to animal anatomy, or mechanical objects (if creating robots etc), helps you to craft creatures that are engaging, weird but still relate to the readers world.

Well, that's great Matt! But how do you actually use reference to make amazing images?

OK, let's have a look at some examples.

When illustrating for kids' books, we normally want to make the characters cute and likeable (even if they are a monster or alien). With this in mind, my approach to using reference usually starts off by roughing out the shapes of the object in its realistic proportions.

Step two, using the drawing I have just created as the reference this time, I then redraw the character, keeping in mind that it is for young children. So I need to amp up the cuteness factor. This can be achieved by changing the head to body proportions, make the head larger, the eyes larger, and the body parts fatter and softer, think of a chubby baby, their forearms are chunky like Popeye, and they have lots of soft rolls.

OK, so that is the basics of using a single reference image to create a standard cute character. But what if you wanted to create a fantasy creature, monster or alien? You're in luck, the process is the same, but instead of using a single reference image, you use multiple and combine them in a way that suits your creation.

Let's examine how we would make a flying frog sitting on a mushroom. Perhaps he is an avatar in a kid's picture book on the environment.

Step one : Create a rough drawing based on a single reference image.

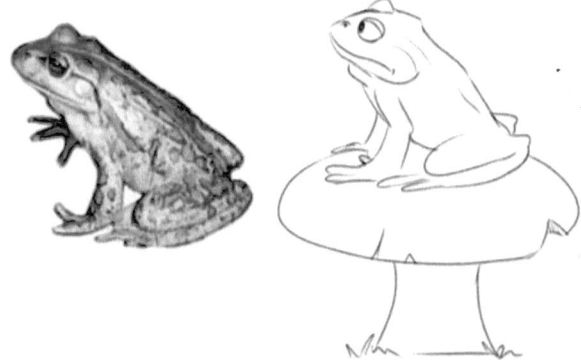

Step 2: Determine the style of wings you want (butterfly, bat, or birds), and find an image to use as reference. You can place the reference together if it helps, or just use it separately. I like to combine where possible. Then repeat step 1. You can keep adding elements as required to create some awesome characters/creatures.

YOUR TURN

Your turn. Let's have a go at using reference to create characters.

MY CHARACTERS

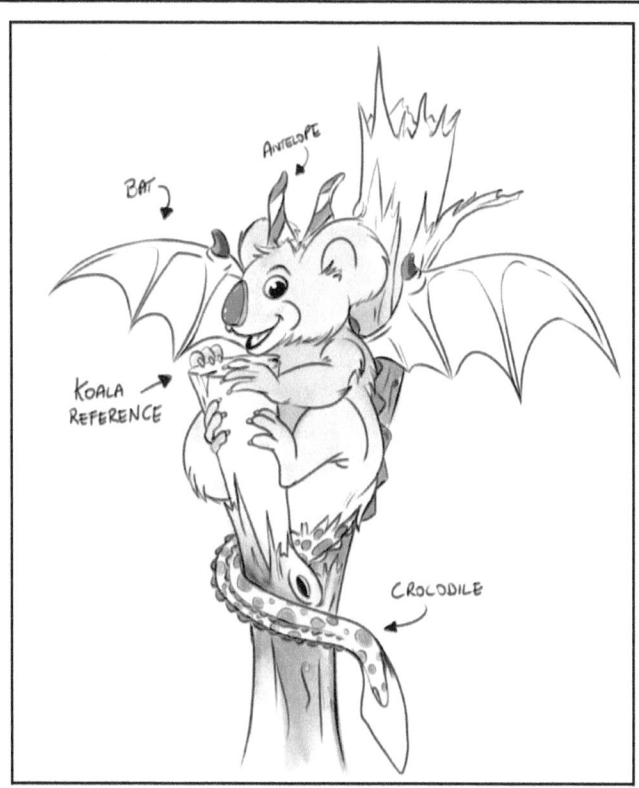

22. COMPOSITION

The most common understanding of composition is the placement or arrangement of the visual elements of your artwork. To make truly amazing art, not only do you need to have correct placement of your elements, but you also need to consider the relationship between each element (juxtaposition), the VALUE/CONTRAST, BALANCE, the RULE OF THIRDS, COLOUR, NEGATIVE SPACE and RHYTHM.

VALUE/CONTRAST:
When you hear the term contrast, you probably think of light and dark, and yes, this is a crucial component of contrast. Using light and dark and the gradations in-between is vital when looking at the value of the overall art work (which we will discuss shortly), but contrast also refers to the relationship between two elements (often referred to as juxtaposition). When looking at the composition of your intended illustration, using contrast in size, colour and tone will improve the visual appeal of the final artwork.

Use of value can also create contrast. Compositions that have a clear contrast have more impact on the viewer. Value refers to the range between black and white. The question of value becomes, where do I place the darkest part of the composition?

VALUE / CONTRAST

Another way to think of composition is balance. I achieve balance by combining the use of colours, the contrast of detail to negative space, even the use of different textural elements or mediums to create the composition.

Here is an activity for you to try. Use different brush strokes and colour to emphasise the balance between active and quiet areas. Put more active markings in the area you want the viewer to focus on, while using broader and softer marks in the areas of calm or less focus. You can achieve this with colour, too. Put more vivid, pure colours where you want the eye to focus and use more neutral colours for the areas of the composition you want the eyes to rest in.

One of the most common mistakes artists can make is to concentrate on one area of detail and then overwork it. Balance comes from working the entire painting and not one area at a time.

Another way to achieve balance and contrast is use of **NEGATIVE SPACE**: Compositions need negative space, or areas of calm to allow the eyes of the viewer to rest.

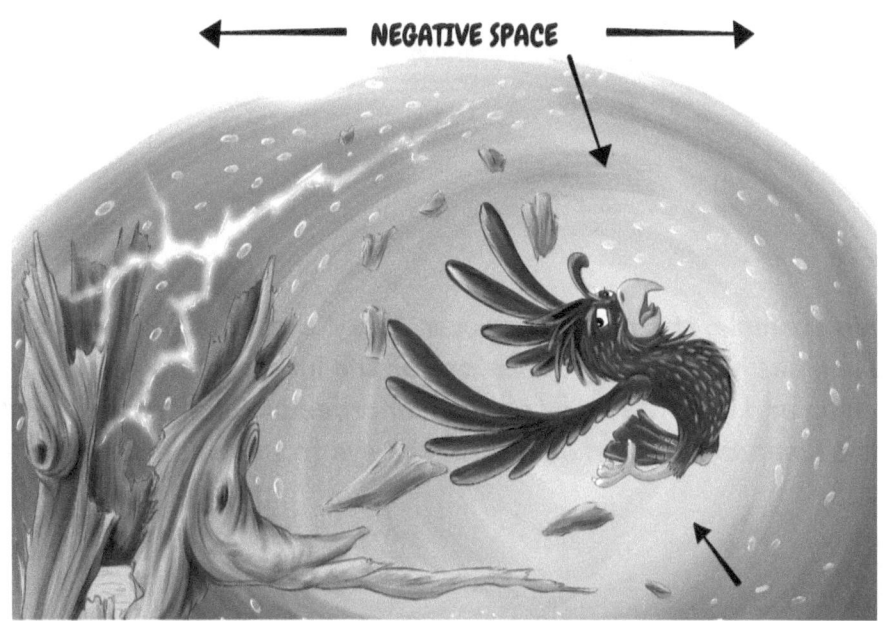

RULE OF THIRDS:

The **RULE OF THIRDS** is a method of creating a **CENTRE OF INTEREST**. A composition works best when there is a clear centre of interest or focal point.

I achieve this by dividing the page in to 3rds horizontally and vertically which creates 4 points of intersection. The primary focus, action, or point of interest should lay close to one or more of these points.

This helps to direct the viewer's eye and create a strong sense of order in your composition.

In this example, the main character, 'Ocky' explodes from his tree. You can see his action crosses one of the intersection points. The lightning and the tree also fringe on or cross an intersecting point. So the composition works to draw the eye from one section to the next.

The last aspect of composition I would like to touch on is Rhythm. Often overlooked, most people only refer to rhythm when talking about writing. But Rhythm has just as important a place in good composition.

I achieve rhythm by using repetition of lines and shapes to create a sense of movement.

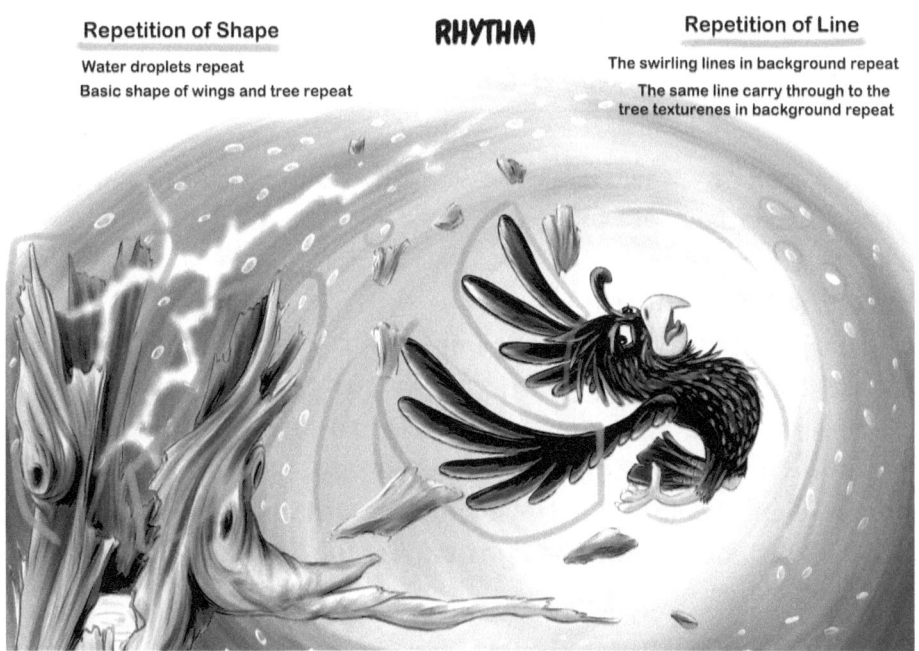

Repetition of Shape
Water droplets repeat
Basic shape of wings and tree repeat

RHYTHM

Repetition of Line
The swirling lines in background repeat
The same line carry through to the tree texturenes in background repeat

Repetition of Line: The swirling lines in the background repeat and the same line carries through to the tree textures.

Repetition of Shape: The water droplets repeat. The basic shape of the wings repeats, same shape for main tree elements.

It is a simple thing to apply to an illustration, but it makes a tremendous difference to the appeal of the final illustration.

23. COVER ART

Why is there a section on cover art I hear you ask? Well the simple answer is this, the book cover is the first thing people see. Obvious right, but think about it, the image, text or message your portray on the cover draws attention (or doesn't) to your book, enough to make a potential reader stop what they are doing and pick up your book.

I have a saying that sums this up:

> The **COVER** is the **HOOK** that **SELLS** your **BOOK!**

So, let's look at a few things you can do to make sure your cover grabs the readers' attention.

CREATE STRONG CONTRAST:
A strong contrast is critically important. You want your reader to read the title easily; you don't want it to disappear into the background. You also want your cover to stand out from other covers in the same genre. Use contrast to exaggerate the light and darks of the imagery. Have the text written in either Light on dark background, or dark on light background so it really pops off the page.

I achieve this by having a lighter background at the top of book (with a dark title) and grading down to a dark background at the bottom of the book (with the author name in white).

The cover should be instantly legible even from a distance.

USE VIVID IMAGERY:
Vivid, striking or funny imagery catches the readers' attention, and that is exactly what you want. Think about the last time you were in a bookshop or browsing the Amazon store for something to buy. There were books you saw that made you stop and want to look at it, even before you read a single line of the blurb.

Getting the reader to 'stop!' is the primary goal of the cover (remember my mantra, it's the HOOK that sells your BOOK)

When deciding on what imagery to use on your cover, think about what element of your story will make the book stand out. You want the reader to stop and think 'WOW, that graphic is exciting', or 'That's an interesting image. I wonder what that book is about?'

Use of colour, composition and typography all help to create a feeling of excitement, intrigue, or fascination about your book.

USE GREAT TYPOGRAPHY:
I mentioned typography, which is just the text you use and it can make or break your book. Choosing the wrong font can make your book look unprofessional, it can cause confusion, for example, if you wrote a book on 'my first day at school' and you use a horror style font like 'Bloody' (although some kids might think the first day of school is a horror story, tee hee).

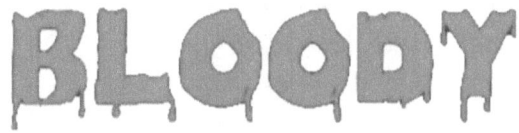

It wouldn't resonate with the parent or carer who is likely to buy the book. The *Type* or *Font* you choose and the way it is set on the cover creates an emotional trigger, and we want the right emotion that suits the genre of the book.

BE RELEVANT TO THE GENRE:
The cover of a book is the window into the story. It should be immediately recognisable. Now if you were writing a horror book, or a romance novel, this would be fairly easy (think Stephen King books or Mills and Boon). With picture books it is still a critical element to consider when designing your cover.

As discussed earlier, there are many types of picture books ranging from board books to illustrated stories. The artwork and typography of your cover needs to be congruent with the intended target audience.

As an example, let's say you have written a children's picture book on dinosaurs aimed at readers 2-5 years of age.

To appeal to them, you would probably use a more cartoonish, vivid, flat colour style illustration that is fun and engaging.

OK, so what if you are writing a dinosaur picture book aimed at readers' 6-9 years of age.

You are more likely to want a semi-realistic style of dinosaur. They can still be relaxed and comical in facial expressions, but the main body of the dinosaur could look fairly realistic.

In most cases, you will probably hire a professional graphic designer who specialises in cover design (it is worth the money as they spend years perfecting their skills), but if you are an author/illustrator and want to do the cover design yourself, then here is an example cover that I created (for a fictional story I may yet write).

It highlights some additional tips to keep in mind when creating your composition, including...

THE RULE OF 3RDS

USE OF WHITE SPACE

CONTINUATION OF ARTWORK (especially for kid's books)

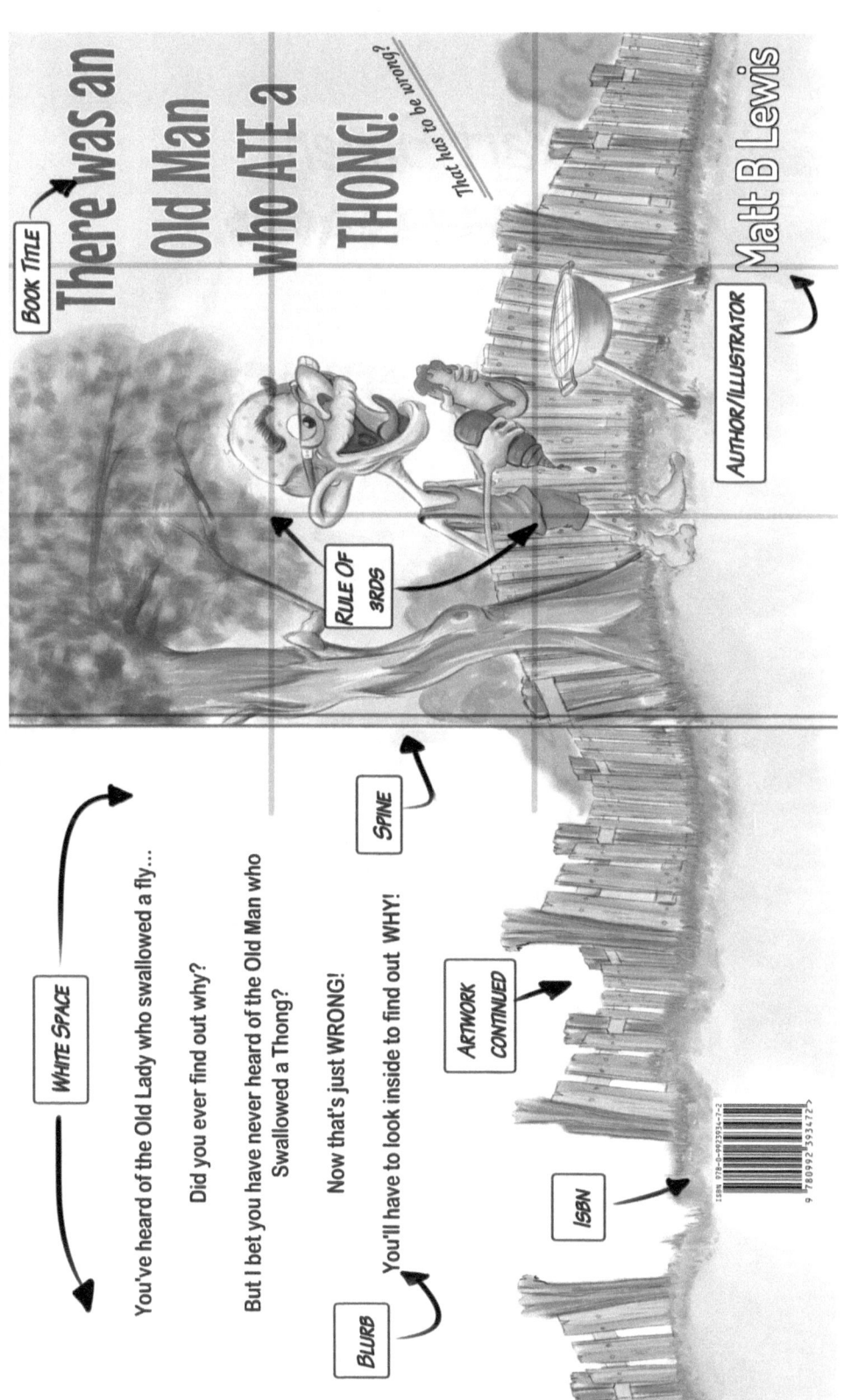

Part Seven
****

A Picture Paints A Thousand Words

24. PORTFOLIO PERFECTION

Almost every illustrator or artist knows what it means when we talk about portfolios. In short, it refers to a collection of art that showcases your best work to date, whether it is painting, drawing, animation or 3D sculpting, it doesn't matter, it's only purpose is to show an art director the style and quality of your work.

For children's books and picture books, what you showcase determines how successful you are at getting contracted for work. There are 3 key elements to a portfolio. Skill, Style and Substance. Skill (that is the drawing, design, render - or technical elements) you will hone over years of practice, they say you need approximately 10000 hours before you are an expert at any skill, so the secret here is practice, practice and practice some more. Style (mediums, artistic choices, illustrators you wish to emulate) is something you develop and can change throughout your career. You may adopt one style for picture books and a different style for chapter books or graphic novels (as I do). However, even if you model yourself after a mentor, an artist you truly admire, your style will still be unique.

What we can focus on here that will help in making you stand out from everyone else is the **SUBSTANCE** of your art. OK, so what do I mean when I say substance?

There is a list of about 20 categories, each with 4 to 5 elements you should include in your portfolio. Now that adds up to almost 100 things, but I am not advocating that you have 100 pieces in your portfolio. Quite the opposite, you should only have 10 - 15 of your strongest pieces in a portfolio.

But there is nothing to say that each illustration can't encompass several categories at once. Creating stunning illustrations that use multiple elements is the method I want you to follow when considering your children's book portfolio.

So what should you have in your portfolio? I'm glad you asked.

THE LIST

1. FORMATS AND SIZES:
Spot illustrations, vignettes, full page and double spreads, negative space (keep room for text), and covers.

2. COLOUR SCHEMES:
Full colour, black and white, and monochrome.

3. LIGHTING: (MOOD)
Morning, noon, evening, night, spotlight, fire, ambient, on camera, on camera hidden, off camera.

4. CHARACTER TYPES: (CONSISTENCY IS VITAL)
Animals, humans, creatures, and objects.

5. AGES:
Children, baby, teens, and (occasionally) adults.

6. GENDER:
Girls, boys, men, and women.

7. EMOTION:
Anger, excitement, happiness, sadness, fear, confidence, curiosity, love, sleeping, pain.

8. SCALE: (CONTRAST)
Large and small, huge objects, tiny objects, vary scale in compositions.

9. RACE:
Asian, Indian, Hispanic, Caucasian, African, Indigenous, multicultural.

10. ANIMALS: (NATURAL OR ANTHROPOMORPHISED)
Amphibians, mammals, fish, reptiles, insects, birds.

11. CREATURES:
Monsters, aliens, robots, dragons, ghosts.

12. ACTIVITIES:
Family, friends, picnics, going to places (beach, shop, zoo).

13. ENVIRONMENTS:
Interiors, exteriors, modern, vintage, ancient, houses, apartments, land, sea, earth, outer-space, dessert, forest, tropical, arctic.

14. SEASONS AND/OR WEATHER:
Winter, spring, summer, autumn,
Wind, rain, lightning, snow, fog, cold, hot.

15. SURFACES:
Shiny, matte, textured, furry, translucent, rough.

16. ACTION:
Falling, breaking, sliding, moving fast, running, jumping, flying, rolling, skidding.

17. CAMERA ANGLES:
Establishing, close ups, medium, distant, high angle, low angle, profile, dynamic, POV.

18. VEHICLES:
Cars, trucks, busses, boats, planes, construction equipment, submarines, space ships.

19. PROPS:
Household items, garage, kitchen, farm, office, food, bathroom, attic, school, games, toys.

20. COMPLEX IMAGES:
Multiple figures, multiple objects.

Part Eight
****

Sorry Not Sorry Important Boring Stuff

25. DOCUMENT SETUP

Document set up can me a couple of things when referring to picture books. If you are primarily a writer and are submitting your story to a literary agent or publisher, then you will focus on the manuscript. If you are self-publishing, then you will want to create PDF ready documents for uploading to either a Print on Demand service like IngramSparks or Kindle Direct Publishing (which I discuss in chapter 27) or to a Printing firm like Imago or Union Printing.

The industry standard for sending your manuscript to AGENTS or PUBLISHERS stipulates they must be:

Typed (doc/x or PDF are the preferred formats)

12 point font size

Times New Roman font

1.5 or Double spaced (paragraph formatting)

Pages should be numbered (picture books usually fit on one page)

Include your name and address (you'll be surprised how often this is omitted)

You can include illustrator notes if absolutely necessary (in italics at end of story)

Often, agents and publishers also require a cover letter to accompany the document.

As always, it pays to do your research on the guidelines for each publisher/agent you want to approach.

Next, let's look at how to set up your document in InDesign.

INDESIGN

So why am I taking the time to delve into the inner workings of using InDesign? Simply put, InDesign is one of the leading software used for the creation of books and magazines, and widely used by publishers and print on demand companies worldwide.

InDesign allows you to set all the document properties from bleeds, to gutters and margins and embedding images and fonts. Yes, there are many other word processing applications you can use, however none with added features that InDesign can leverage.

Once you have your manuscript set up, not only can you create print ready pdf files for sending to publishers or printers. You can also export to **Interactive PDF, EPUB** (for eBooks), **Flash** (for animated books), and even output to **Word**.

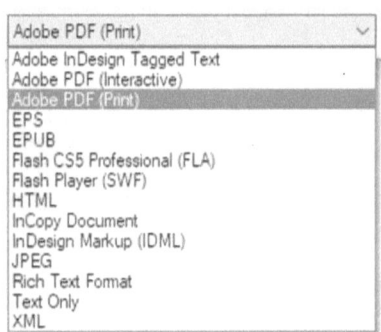

So let's walk through setting up your InDesign document to create your picture book. I will also take the time now to apologise if you (the reader) feel this is teaching you something you already know, or is a waste of time. I have included it in this book because it accounts for a lot of my time when working with a client.

In almost every case, once they have created the manuscript, they then engage me to set up the document for them so they can send to either a printer, publisher or print on demand company.

Hopefully this little section will save you a lot of time and money in the future.

Open InDesign, go to File_New

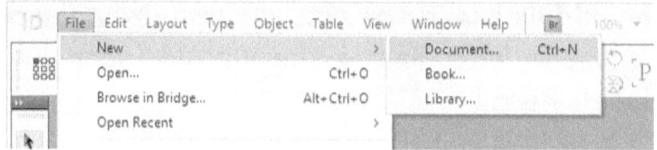

The New Document window opens. Let's work through each important section in this window.

NUMBER OF PAGES: As it shows this is where we add the number of internal pages for our book. (If self-publishing/ printing, you need two documents, one with internal pages and a second one for the cover).

PAGE SIZE: This is where you set the physical size of your finished book (once printed and trimmed)

MARGIN: the margin is the guides inside the page where the important information must sit. Most Print on Demand companies have a matrix to work this out. As an example, if your book is 32 pages at 216mm X 216mm then the margin should be 9.6mm.

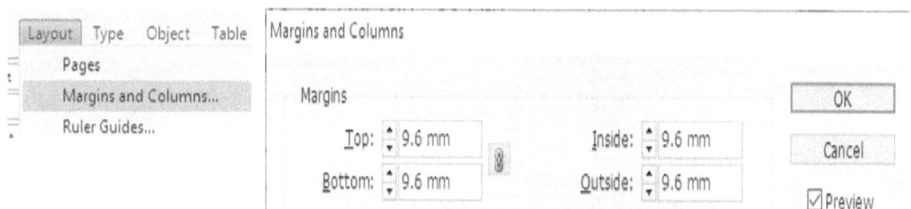

BLEED: The bleed is the amount added to the page for you to extend the artwork in case of inaccuracies in the trimming process it is normally 3mm or 5mm. Once done click OK.

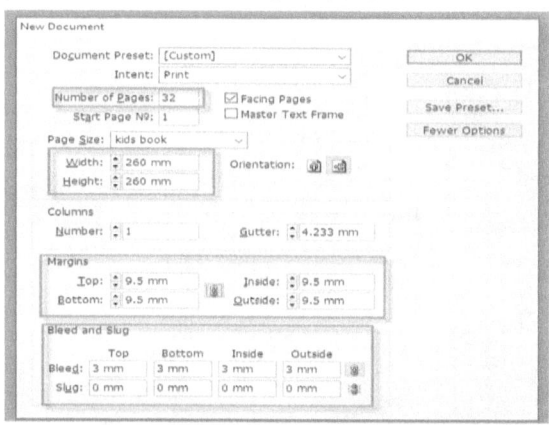

You've created an InDesign document. The outer line is the bleed setting, the middle line is the actual page size once printed and trimmed, and the inner line is the margin (keep all important elements inside here.)

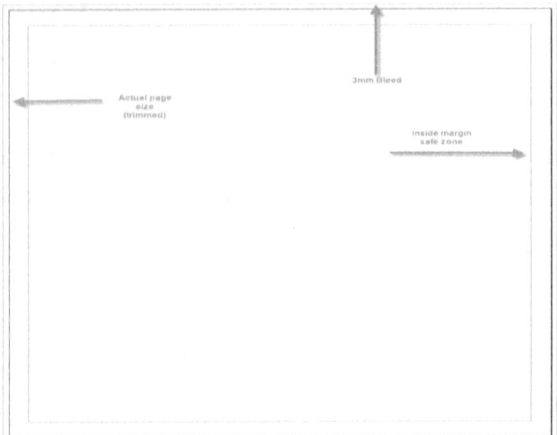

To add your images, go to File_Place...

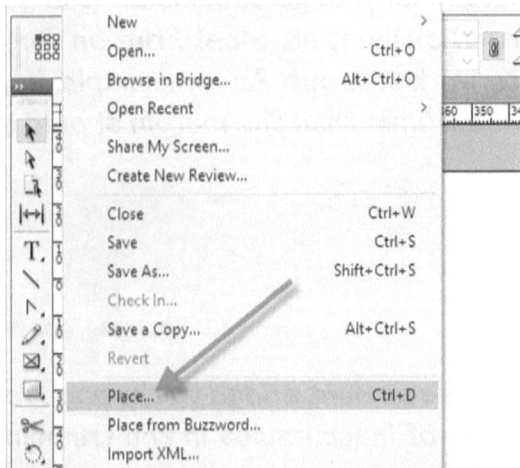

Use the look in drop-down to navigate to where you have all your artwork stored.

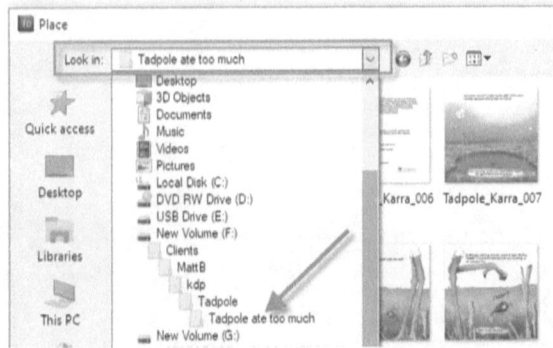

Select the first image, and click on open. You will need to do each page one at a time.

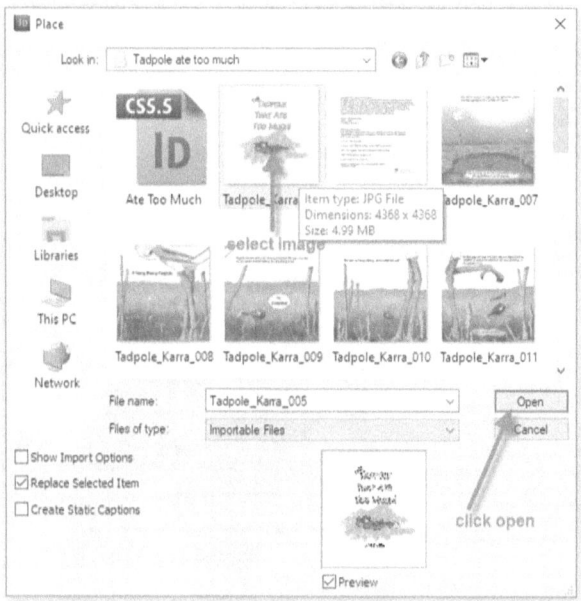

It is important to create your artwork to the dimensions of your page (with bleed) so it fits exactly. If you need to resize (which isn't the best practice), you double click the image so the border changes to red, resize image. Then click off and single click image to adjust the blue line (which is a mask) to make sure nothing is getting hidden.

Repeat this process for all pages.

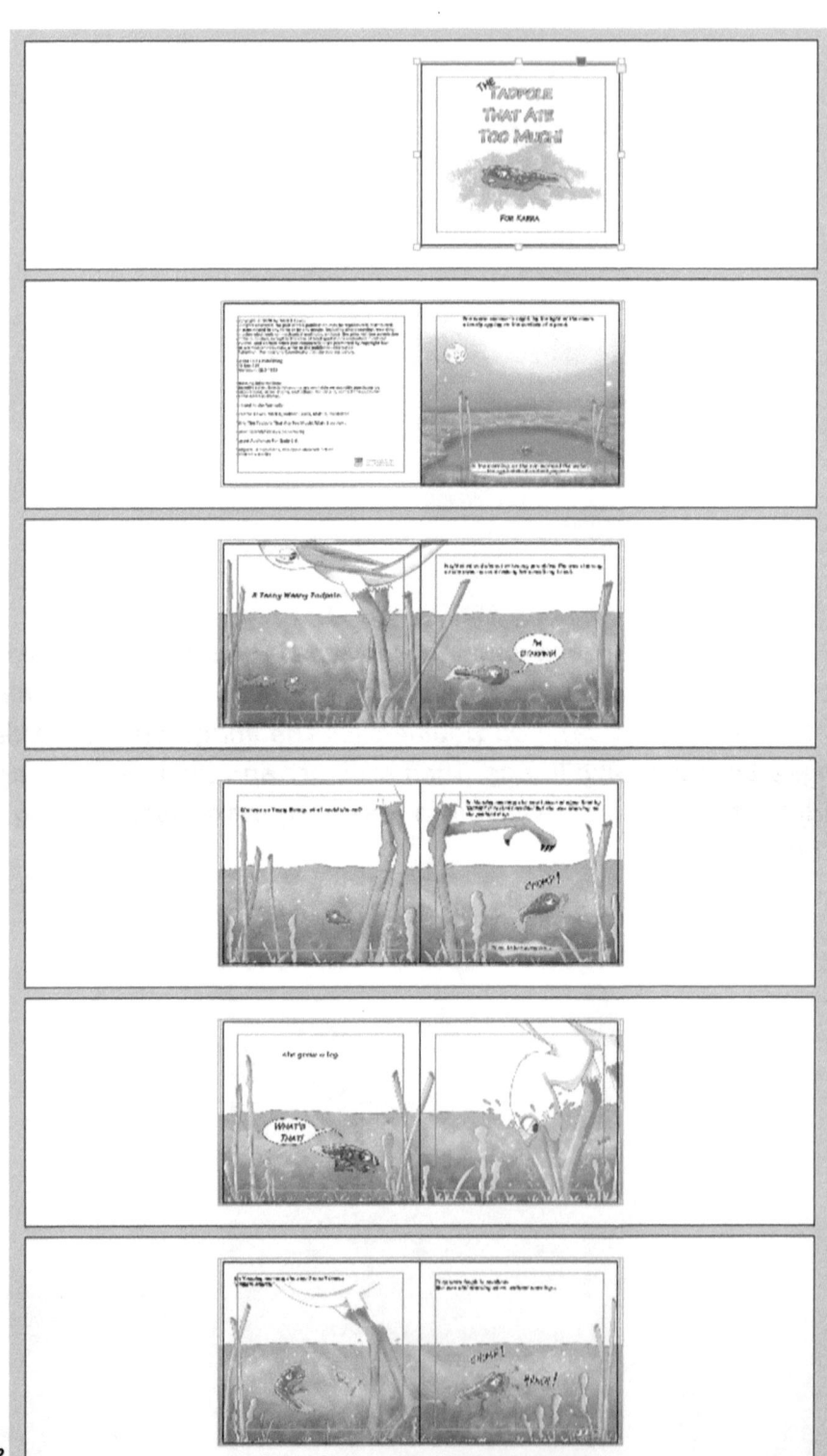

When you are happy with your document and you want to create a PDF to upload to a Print on demand or to send to a printer, click File_Adobe PDF Preset, and select [PDF/X-1a:2001]...

Select the file location to save the PDF to.

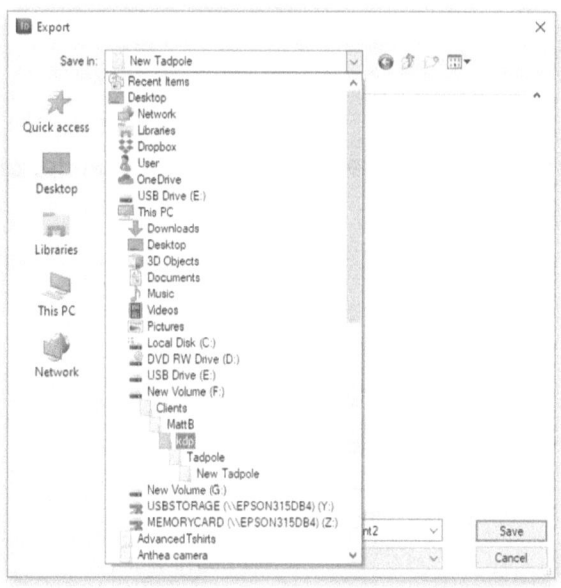

Unless you have specific instructions from the printer/publisher, accept the defaults and click export. Depending on the size of your document and the image resolution of the artwork, this might take a few minutes.

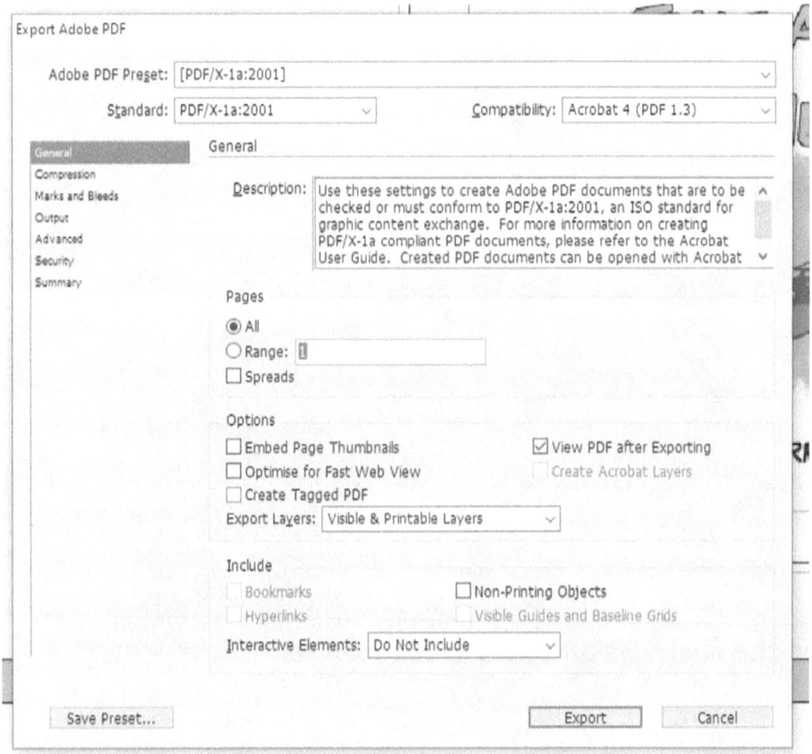

Depending on your settings the PDF may open up, or it will simply be saved to your folder.

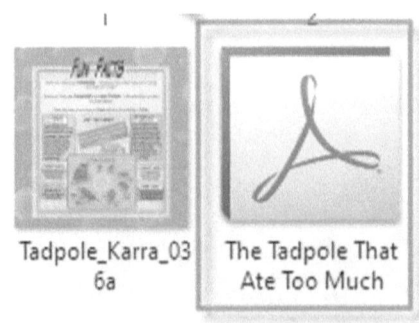

Part Nine
****

Publish Or Print That Is The Question?

26. PATH TO PUBLICATION

You have accomplished everything! Well, almost you have written an amazing manuscript and perhaps even had it illustrated. So what's left to do?

To hold the book in your hand or to share it with family, friends or the rest of the world, you need to get it PUBLISHED. There are several paths to publication, TRADITIONAL, SELF-PRINT, PRINT ON DEMAND, or a LITERARY AGENT. The Holy Grail for most writers is to have their book published by one of the big 5 publishing houses. Scholastic, Penguin Random House, Hachette, Allen & Unwin, or Pan Macmillan.

And, while to be published by one of them would be outstanding, there are many wonderful publishing houses available to the budding writer and/or illustrator.

I have compiled a list of Australian publishers specifically accepting picture book submissions. I will also include a list of international publishers accepting manuscripts. You will still need to do your research on each to determine those accepting picture books and ones that publish similar to your style.

Most of the major publishers don't accept unsolicited manuscripts. By this I mean they only accept manuscripts from literary agents or authors currently in their stable. Occasionally they may open for a small window for unsolicited submissions, but generally the larger publishing houses are very difficult to get into.

So, how do you submit to a publisher? The very first step is to look at the publisher's website, and look at their submission guidelines. They all have them. Some will say closed to submissions, others will identify how they want the manuscripts formatted, and how they want them received.

Most publishers have a form or accept submissions only through digital communications.

Submission Guidelines:

For a Picture Book, publishers will often ask for the entire manuscript, as well as a synopsis, and a cover letter and possibly three to four illustrations (if you are both illustrator and author). They will also ask for your publishing history, if any, and what they refer to as Comps. Comps are a comparison of your book to similar books in the marketplace.

Publishers like to see how your picture book is similar to and unique from other books in the market. It gives them an idea of how well the book will perform and helps them decide if they should invest in your book.

If a publisher accepts your Picture Book, they take on all the risk— they pay for every facet of book production: editing, layout, design, marketing, etc.

The important thing to remember here is that the author makes no financial investment in the production of their book. In return, you would get an advance (or an advance against royalties, in which case sales of the book have to pay back the publisher's advance before you receive any royalty payments), and royalties anywhere from 7 to 12%.

Usually, book production will take anywhere between 18 and 24 months. Even if accepted by a publisher, there are certain expectations that the author will also do their own marketing and promotion. Having a good social network will help in this endeavour.

Facebook   Linkedin   Instagram   Twitter   Youtube

Another time saving trick is to have a Submission Kit ready in advance. It should contain templates for:
Cover Letter - a brief letter to an editor outlining your book.
Title Sheet - attaches to your manuscript.
Author Bio - written in 3rd person; this outlines who you are as an author.
In today's digital world, they usually ask for this as a single email submission. Following is an actual submission I sent to a publisher.

SAMPLE SUBMISSION

Dear Acquisitions Editor

My name is Matt B Lewis. I am an author/illustrator of children's books and I enclose a picture book text for your consideration.

THE TADPOLE THAT ATE TOO MUCH! (375 words), written for children approximately 5-7 years old.

It's a fun story which describes the life cycle of an amphibian. The story centres on the struggles of a single tadpole, as she deals with hunger and changes in her body, and the ending has a funny twist.

COMPS: This book is similar to Eric Carle's 'The Hungry Caterpillar' in so far as it tracks the life cycle of a tadpole.

It is unique in its story, illustration and the surprise ending. It also contains a STEM sheet at the end of the book.

I intend to use the last page for a fact sheet on frogs/toads which supports STEM related activities.

As requested in your Call for Submissions, I have attached 4 illustrated pages (as 2 double spreads) to show the style I would use to complete this book and a rough storyboard of the action and page turns.

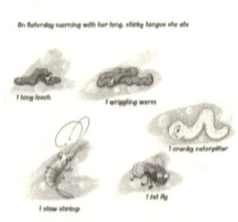

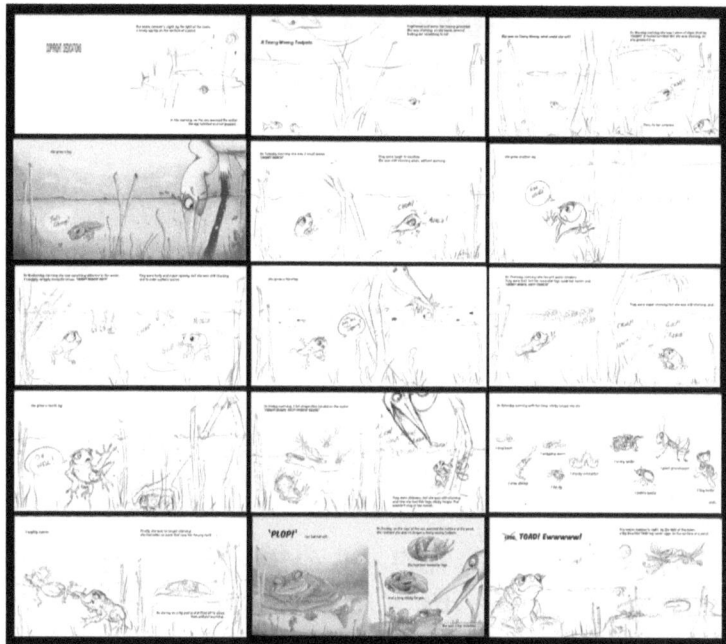

Thank you in advance for reviewing my manuscript. I hope you enjoy the story.

I look forward to hearing from you as any feedback you can offer will be most valuable.

I have several other manuscripts available should you wish to see more of my work.

https://mattblewis.com/

https://asastylefile.com/illustrator/matt-b-lewis/
https://www.scbwi.org/members-public/matthew-lewis
https://www.instagram.com/matt.b.illustrations/
https://www.facebook.com/MattB.Illustrations
https://www.linkedin.com/in/mrmattblewis/
https://twitter.com/MrMattB
https://www.youtube.com/channel/UCq8nsNSHA3_NmfffOUcHCDQ/

Matt B Lewis Illustrator and Author

SAMPLE COVER LETTER

Name of editor
Editor title (e.g. Commissioning Editor) Children's Books
Company name
Address
Date

Dear Ms. ABC,

I enclose a picture book text for your consideration.

THE TADPOLE THAT AT TOO MUCH, written for children of approximately grade 3-4. It's a fun story which describes the life cycle of an amphibian. The story centers on the struggles of a single tadpole, as she deals with hunger and changes in her body. The ending has an unexpected twist.

Thank you in advance for reviewing my manuscript. I hope you enjoy the story. I look forward to hearing from you as any feedback you can offer will be most valuable.

I also have several other manuscripts available should you wish to see more of my work. Thank you for your time.

Best wishes,

Matt B Lewis

Address

Tel/mobile
Email address
Website

SAMPLE TITLE SHEET

THE TADPOLE THAT ATE TOO MUCH
by
MATT B LEWIS
Address, telephone number, email address
(Insert)

THE TADPOLE THAT ATE TOO MUCH, written for children of approximately grade 3-4. It's a fun story which describes the life cycle of an amphibian. The story centres on the struggles of a single tadpole, as she deals with hunger and changes in her body... the ending has a funny and unexpected twist.

All aspects have been thoroughly research and written to have kids asking questions. The last page contains information on frogs and toads which supports STEM related activities.

454 words
Possible illustration notes in italics
(Insert as required)

SAMPLE AUTHOR BIO

MATT B LEWIS (ILLUSTRATOR AND AUTHOR)

When not battling 'Bunyip's', dodging 'Drop Bears', or wrestling 'Yowies' in the Australian bush, Matt B spends his time writing and illustrating children's books.

A welcome guest at schools and creative events, Matt B inspires and empowers children through his foundational approach to illustration, storytelling and creative character design.

An Amazon Best-Selling Author, Matt B has written and/or illustrated over 20 books with kangaroos, wombats and echidnas, he's always on the lookout to illustrate some coyotes, buffalos, and groundhogs.

Matt B is passionate about Education and the Environment and holds a Bachelor's Degree in Further Education and Training and a Master's Degree in Environmental and Business Management.

Matt B lives, plays, and creates in Queensland, Australia with his wife and two amazingly creative kids.

Let's talk **AUTHOR BIOS**, you should have a template for 3 different styles. The **SHORT BIO** (one liner)-for signature block, social media posts, the **STANDARD BIO** (100 - 150 words) for sending to publishers, agents etc, and a **LONG FORM BIO** (300 words) for media releases or articles on you as a creative.

YOUR TURN!

Here's your time to shine. Remember to sell yourself in the 3rd person, as if someone is telling the world how **AMAZING** you are:

SHORT BIO

STANDARD BIO

149

AUSTRALIAN PUBLISHERS ACCEPTING PICTURE BOOKS

Affirm Press
http://affirmpress.com.au/submissions/
Picture book submissions only accepted first Monday of the month

Big Sky Publishing
https://www.bigskypublishing.com.au/about-us/submitting-a-manuscript/

Bloomsbury Spark
https://www.bloomsbury.com/au/bloomsbury-spark/submissions

Christmas Press
https://christmaspresspicturebooks.com/submissions/

DoctorZed
https://www.doctorzed.com/submissions/

EK Books
http://ekbooks.org/submissions

Empowering Resources
http://www.empoweringresources.com.au/new-submissions/

Ethicool Books
https://ethicoolbooks.com

Ford Street
http://www.fordstreetpublishing.com/ford/index.php/about-fordstreet/submissions

Hardie Grant Egmont
https://www.hardiegrant.com/au/hardie-grant-childrens-publishing/about/submissions

IP Kidz
https://www.ipoz.biz/ip-kidz/
We're open from March – December

Larrikin House
https://www.larrikinhouse.com/submissions

New Frontier
https://www.newfrontier.com.au/submission-guidelines

New Holland Publishers
http://au.newhollandpublishers.com/submissions

Odyssey Books
http://odysseybooks.com.au/submissions/

Pademelon Press
http://www.pademelonpress.com.au/information-for-authors/

Penguin Random House
https://penguin.com.au/getting-published/children
Picture book submissions are open from 1 April to 30 November.

Red Paper Kite
https://www.redpaperkite.com/submissions
RED paper kite's focus is on children's picture books. That's all we do.

Starfish Bay
http://starfishbaypublishing.com.au/submissions/

Thames & Hudson
https://thamesandhudson.com.au/contact/getting-published/

Wild Orange
https://wildorangepublishing.com/submissions/

Wombat Books
http://www.wombatbooks.com.au/authors/submissions

Yellow Brick Books
http://www.yellowbrickbooks.com.au/submissions.html

OTHER PUBLISHERS ACCEPTING MANUSCRIPTS

1. HOLIDAY HOUSE
Website: www.holidayhouse.com
Submission Guidelines: www.holidayhouse.com/faqs

2. ARBORDALE PUBLISHING
Website: www.arbordalepublishing.com
Submission Guidelines: www.arbordalepublishing.com/submission-guidelines

3. IMMEDIUM
Website: www.immedium.com
Submission Guidelines: www.immedium.com/submission-guidelines

4. LEE & LOW BOOKS
Website: www.leeandlow.com
Submission Guidelines: www.leeandlow.com/submission-guidelines

5. EKLAVYA
Website: www.eklavya.in
Submission Guidelines: www.eklavya.in

6. ALBERT WHITMAN & COMPANY
Website: www.albertwhitman.com
Submission Guidelines: www.albertwhitman.com/submission-guidelines

7. CHARLESBRIDGE PUBLISHING
Website: www.charlesbridge.com
Submission Guidelines: www.charlesbridge.com/submission-guidelines

8. FREE SPIRIT PUBLISHING
Website: www.freespirit.com
Submission Guidelines: www.freespirit.com/submission-guidelines

9. LITTLE TIGER PRESS
Website: www.littletiger.co.uk
Submission Guidelines: www.littletiger.co.uk/submission-guidelines

10. WORKMAN PUBLISHING
Website: www.workman.com
Submission Guidelines: www.workman.com/submission-guidelines

11. KANE MILLER
Website: www.friends.kanemiller.com
Submission Guidelines: www.friends.kanemiller.com/submission-guidelines

12. PANTS ON FIRE PRESS
Website: www.pantsonfirepress.com
Submission Guidelines: www.pantsonfirepress.com/submission-guidelines

13. TILBURY HOUSE PUBLISHERS
Website: www.tilburyhouse.com
Submission Guidelines: www.tilburyhouse.com/submission-guidelines

14. ONSTAGE PUBLISHING
Website: www.onstagepublishing.com
Submission Guidelines: www.onstagepublishing.com/submission-guidelines

15. ABDO PUBLISHING
Website: www.abdopublishing.com
Submission Guidelines: www.abdobooks.com/submission-guidelines

16. ABRAMS BOOK
Website: www.abramsbooks.com
Submission Guidelines: www.abramsbooks.com/submission-guidelines

17. ALLIGATOR BOOKS
Website: www.alligatorbooks.co.uk
Submission Guidelines:

18. ALLEN AND UNWIN
Website: www.allenandunwin.com
Submission Guidelines: www.allenandunwin.com/submission-guidelines

19. ALBERT WHITMAN
Website: www.albertwhitman.com
Submission Guidelines: www.albertwhitman.com/submission-guidelines

20. ANNICK PRESS
Website: www.annickpress.com
Submission Guidelines: www.annickpress.com/submission-guidelines

21. ANDERSEN PRESS
Website: www.andersenpress.co.uk
Submission Guidelines: www.andersenpress.co.uk/submission-guidelines

22. ANDREWS MCMEEL
Website: www.andrewsmcmeel.com
Submission Guidelines: www.publishing.andrewsmcmeel.com/submission-guidelines

23. AZBOOKS
Website: www.azbooksusa.com
Guidelines: www.azbooksusaconsumer.com/submission-guidelines

24. Barefoot books
Website: www.barefootbooks.com
Submission Guidelines: www.barefootbooks.com/submission-guidelines

25. Barron's Educational Series
Website: www.barronsbooks.com
Submission Guidelines: www.barronbooks.com/submission-guidelines

26. Bloomsbury
Website: www.bloomsbury.com
Submission Guidelines: www.bloomsbury.com/submission-guidelines

27. Blue Apple Books
Website: www.blueapplebooks.com
Submission Guidelines: www.blueapplebooks.com/submission-guidelines

28. Boxer books
Website: www.boxerbooksltd.co.uk
Submission Guidelines: www.boxerbooksltd.co.uk/submission-guidelines

29. Buster Books
Website: www.busterbooks.co.uk
Submission Guidelines: www.mombooks.com/submission-guidelines

30. Capstone
Website: www.capstonepub.com
Submission Guidelines: www.capstonepub.com/submission-guidelines

31. Caramel tree
Website: www.carameltree.com
Submission Guidelines: www.carameltree.com/submission-guidelines

32. Cheeky Monkey Publishing
Website: www.cheekymonkeypublishing.com
Submission Guidelines:

33. Chronicle Books
Website: www.chroniclebooks.com
Guidelines: www.chroniclebooks.com/submission-guidelines

34. Curious Fox
Website: www.curious-fox.com
Submission Guidelines: www.curious-fox.com/submission-guidelines

35. Chicken House
Website: www.chickenhousebooks.com
Submission Guidelines: www.chickenhousebooks.com/submission-guidelines

36. Epigram Books
Website: www.epigrambooks.sg
Submission Guidelines: www.shop.epigrambooks.sg/submission-guidelines

37. Eerdmans
Website: www.eerdmans.com
Submission Guidelines: www.eerdmans.com/submission-guidelines

38. Fat Fox Books
Website: www.fatfoxbooks.com
Submission Guidelines: www.fatfoxbooks.com/submission-guidelines

39. Floris Books
Website: www.florisbooks.co.uk
Submission Guidelines: www.florisbooks.co.uk/submission-guidelines

40. Flying Eye Books
Website: www.flyingeyebooks.com
Submission Guidelines: www.flying-eye/submission-guidelines

41. Goelette International
Website: www.goeletteinternational.com
Submission Guidelines: www.goeletteinternational.com/submission-guidelines

42. Hachette US
Website: www.hachettebookgroup.com
Submission Guidelines: www.hachettebookgroup.com/submission-guidelines

43. HarperCollins
Website: www.harpercollins.co.uk
Submission Guidelines: www.harpercollins.com/submission-guidelines

44. Hinkler Books
Website: www.hinklerbooks.com
Guidelines: www.hinkler.com.au/submission-guidelines

45. HayHouse
Website: www.hayhouse.com
Submission Guidelines: www.hayhouse.com/submission-guidelines

46. Houghton Mifflin Harcourt
Website: www.hmhco.com
Submission Guidelines: www.hmhco.com/submission-guidelines

47. Hogs Back Books
Website: www.hogsbackbooks.com
Submission Guidelines: www.hogsbackbooks.com/submission-guidelines

48. Lion Hudson
Website: www.lionhudson.com
Submission Guidelines: www.lionhudson.com/submission-guidelines

49. Little Tiger
Website: www.littletiger.co.uk
Submission Guidelines: www.littletiger.co.uk/submission-guidelines

50. Lake Press
Website: www.lakepress.com.au
Submission Guidelines: www.lakepress.com.au/submission-guidelines

51. Laurence King
Website: www.laurenceking.com
Submission Guidelines: www.laurenceking.com/submission-guidelines

52. Magination Press
Website: www.apa.org/pubs/magination
Submission Guidelines: www.apa.org/pubs/magination/submission-guidelines

53. Mathew Price
Website: www.mathewprice.com
Submission Guidelines: www.mathewprice.com/submission-guidelines

54. Mighty Media Press
Website: www.mightymediapress.com
Submission Guidelines: www.mightymediapress.com/submission-guidelines

55. New Frontier
Website: www.newfrontier.com.au
Submission Guidelines: www.newfrontier.com.au/submission-guidelines

56. Nosy Crow
Website: www.nosycrow.com
Submission Guidelines: www.nosycrow.com/contact/submissions/

57. Octopus Books
Website: www.octopusbooks.co.uk
Submission Guidelines: www.octopusbooks.net/submission-guidelines

58. Priddy Books
Website: www.priddybooks.com
Submission Guidelines: www.priddybooks.com/submission-guidelines

59. Peter Pauper Press
Website: www.peterpauper.com
Submission Guidelines: www.peterpauper.com/submission-guidelines

60. Random House
Website: www.randomhousechildrens.co.uk
Submission Guidelines: www.penguinrandomhouse.biz/submission-guidelines

61. Really Decent Books
Website: www.reallydecentbooks.co.uk
Submission Guidelines: www.reallydecentbooks.co.uk/submission-guidelines

62. Rockpool Childrens Books
Website: www.rockpoolchildrensbooks.com
Submission Guidelines: www.rockpoolpublishing.com.au/submission-guidelines

63. Simon and Schuster
Website: www.simonandschuster.com
Submission Guidelines: www.simonandschuster.biz/submission-guidelines

64. Sterling Publishing
Website: www.sterlingpublishing.com
Submission Guidelines: www.sterlingpublishing.com/submission-guidelines

65. Storytime Magazine
Website: www.storytimemagazine.com
Submission Guidelines: www.storytimemagazine.com/submission-guidelines

66. Templar
Website: www.templarco.co.uk
Submission Guidelines: www.templarco.co.uk/submission-guidelines

67. The Book Company
Website: www.thebookcompany.com.au
Submission Guidelines: www.thegoodbook.com/submission-guidelines

68. Thames and Hudson
Website: www.thamesandhudson.com
Submission Guidelines: www.thamesandhudson.com/submission-guidelines

69. Imagine That Publishing
Website: www.imaginethat.com
Submission Guidelines: www.imaginethat.com/submission-guidelines

70. Tuttle Publishing
Website: www.tuttlepublishing.com
Submission Guidelines: www.tuttlepublishing.com/submission-guidelines

71. QED Publishing
Website: www.qed-publishing.co.uk
Submission Guidelines: www.quartoknows.com/submission-guidelines

72. Usborne
Website: www.usborne.com
Submission Guidelines: www.usborne.com/submission-guidelines

73. Walker
Website: www.walker.co.uk
Submission Guidelines: www.walker.co.uk/submission-guidelines

74. Workman
Website: www.workman.com
Submission Guidelines: www.workman.com/submission-guidelines

27. SELF-PUBLISH

Self-Publishing used to have a horrible stigma attached. There is a misconception that if you self-publish you are a failure as an author. In today's market, it is a legitimate way to publish.

There are two main approaches to Self-Publishing; one is to hire a print service, and the other is to use a print on demand service.

PRINT SERVICES: are any printer that can print large volumes of books using offset printers. You prepare all your files for the printer specifications and send them the files. Once printed, the printer sends your order to you and then it is up to you to market and sell the books either through booksellers or online marketplaces.

Let's look at the Pros and Cons for using a print service.

PROS:
- Lower cost per book
- Higher quality production values, especially for full-colour books
- You'll have plenty of print copies around

CONS:
- Upfront investment is considerable. In most instances, Print Services have a minimum run order (1000 books) so the initial cost can start at around $3000, which includes the printing and shipping costs. If you use a Print Services located offshore (like China or Korea) you will also have to include custom charges.
- Increased risk—what happens once you have printed 2000 books, what if the books don't sell or you want to put out a new edition before the old one is sold out?
- Shipping costs - if you have ordered 2000 books and you have them warehoused and then you sell them online, you will need to take care of all the logistics involved in packaging and shipping the books to the customer.

The following sections are a quick overview of some of the main avenues for Self-Publishing.

IngramSpark

https://www.ingramspark.com/

To use IngramSpark you need to create an account, don't worry, it's free to set up. Simply click on the sign up link under the login button and follow the prompts.

Once you have created your account and logged in, there are three sections in the menu that will be of most interest for you. At least at the start. They are the **TITLES** section, the **ORDERS** section, and the **HELP** section.

The All Titles lists all the books you have uploaded to IngramSparks, including both print and eBook.

The main one here to look at, especially for a new author, is the Add Title.

They offer you 3 options, Print & eBook, Print Book Only or eBook only. Looking at the cost (which is in USD) you would think it smarter to go with both Print & eBook, which saves you money. However, if you choose this option you need to have the files for both books ready to upload together. The system won't let you just launch the print book now and then come back to the eBook later.

Do you have files ready to upload?

Yes, all my files are ready

No, I would like to see the available options for creating files

No, but I will enter my title information and submit files later

Great! That means you have the following properly-formatted files (please check each box below):

* ☐ Print jacket and/or cover (spread including front, spine, and back cover)(.pdf)
* ☐ Print interior (.pdf)
* ☐ Ebook cover (.jpg)  **You will need these files ready before you can proceed**
* ☐ Ebook interior (.epub)

If you are unsure if your files are properly formatted, please reference our file creation guide for print files or EPUB guidelines for ebook files. If you do not have the required files you may use the IngramSpark book-building tool to create both a cover and interior file (single part file creation is currently not available) by choosing *"No, I would like to see the available options for creating files"* or you can continue by choosing *"No, but I will enter my title information and submit files later"*. You may proceed to add book information, but will need all required files to complete the file upload process.

What would you like to do?

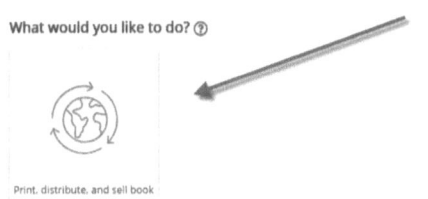

This is the benefit of using IngramSpark, the global distribution allows your book to be sold in a greater number of locations

Print, distribute, and sell book

PRINT INFORMATION
TITLE
LANGUAGE
PRINT ISBN (13 digits)
EBOOK ISBN (13 digits)
PUBLISHING RIGHTS (you own copyright or is it public domain)
AUTHORS & CONTRIBUTORS
CONTRIBUTOR #1:

CATEGORISE YOUR TITLE
SELECT IMPRINT
SUBJECTS (3 subjects maximum)

SELECT AUDIENCE (textbook, Juvenile, Professional, Trade/General (adult) or YA)
TITLE DESCRIPTION
FULL DESCRIPTION (200 - 4000 bytes)

KEYWORDS (Separate with semicolons)

Things you will need to know when completing the setup of your book:

TRIM SIZE:
INTERIOR COLOUR AND PAPER
BINDING
COVER FINISH
PAGE COUNT
PRICING OF YOUR BOOK
DISCOUNT PERCENTAGE FOR WHOLESALERS
RETURNS POLICY

Once you have all the details filled out, it is time to upload your PDF files. (I discuss how to create the PDF files in chapter 25 Document Setup)

You will need a PDF file for the cover and a separate PDF file for the interior pages file. To get the cover file set out correctly, go to the HELP section, and under file creation tools, there is a link to COVER TEMPLATE GENERATOR. Click on the link and fill out the required information and choose InDesign, IDML or PDF for the file type. They will email it to you to add your cover art to it the same way we do in chapter 25 for the interior files.

Once you upload your Cover and Interior PDF files, the system checks (validates) they are technically correct. Then you wait for 1-3 days for IngramSpark to process your files and send you a digital proof. If you are happy with the way the proof looks, you can approve the files and **WHALLA!** You've published your book and set it for global distribution.

You can make minor tweaks to your book once published, add something to the cover, fix a mistake inside the book etc, just upload new files and IngramSpark will make the changes without disruption to your sales channels. If, however, it is a major change, like different illustrations or cover, they consider it a new book and require a new ISBN and a repeat of the original process.

Kindle Direct Publishing (KDP)
https://kdp.amazon.com/en_US/

One of the greatest benefits to using KDP is that it is free to set up as opposed to IngramSpark who charge $49 USD. Second, for eBooks, there is no requirement for an ISBN with KDP.

Why does this help an aspiring Picture Book Author? Speed to the marketplace, you can upload and publish your book in as little as 30 minutes once you have all your files ready. This means you can promote your latest kid's book as an eBook and get reviews within hours, not days or weeks.

KDP doesn't have the same global distribution as IngramSpark, but it is an excellent channel to promote your book. In fact, when I work with clients, I often suggest they publish on both platforms. IngramSpark for the distribution and KDP for the availability (makes your book always available on Amazon) and for speed to market.

It is so easy to publish on KDP as they provide all the tools you need - **Free of Charge.**

So let's have a quick look at what information and or tools you need. As with everything you will need to sign up for an account, again don't worry, it is free.

Sign into your account and choose the format of book you want to start with under the 'Create a New Title' section.

I like to work through the eBook first, get it published and promoted, then go back in to create the print book. But you can do either first.

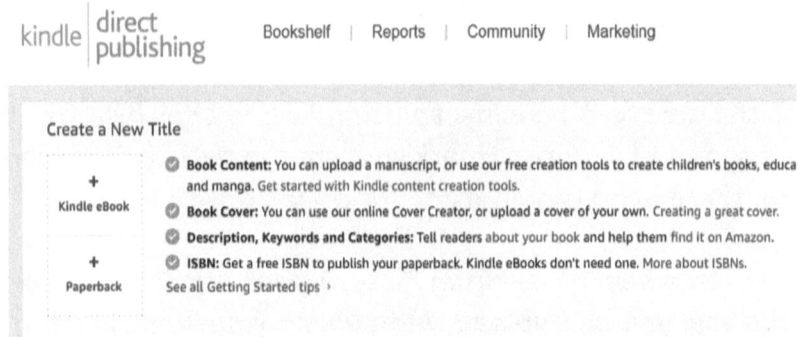

There are three main Kindle creation tools that you can use depending on the type of book you are publishing. **KINDLE CREATE, KINDLE KID'S BOOK CREATOR,** and **KINDLE COMIC CREATOR.** Now as we are focusing on kid's picture books, you can use either Kindle Create or Kindle Kid's Book Creator. I normally just use Kindle Create because I don't add the pop up features, but try each one and see which works best for you. The following diagram shows the essential work flows for each format.

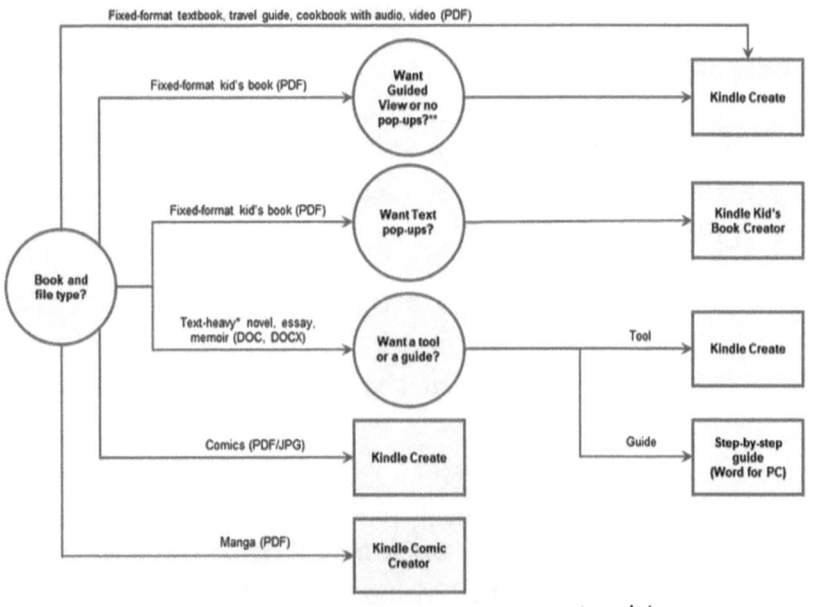

courtesy kdp.amazomn.com

As with other platforms, KDP will require the standard information about the book you are publishing.

LANGUAGE
BOOK TITLE (IS IT A SERIES)
PRINT ISBN (13 digits)
EBOOK (NO ISBN NEEDED)
Edition #
AUTHORS & CONTRIBUTORS
DESCRIPTION (4000 characters)
PUBLISHING RIGHTS (you own copyright or is it public domain)
KEYWORDS
CATEGORIES
AGE AND GRADE RANGE

Once you have completed the metadata, you will go through to the upload your manuscript (for the eBook you need to create an EPUB file using one of the previously mentioned tools) and your cover image (as a JPG or TIFF file). There is the option to preview the book before proceeding to pricing and publishing. I strongly recommend previewing it.

One thing to note about the Print version of the book when uploading. They prefer the internal pages to be in a PDF format, and you will need to have the document set up with the correct bleed and margins. I cover this in chapter 25 Document set up. It takes a day or two to go live, but then you can sell and promote it.

KDP also offers an 'order author copies' feature. You only pay printing and postage cost, it is definitely worth doing to check the quality of your printed book.

Print Services

As mentioned earlier, Print Services are another avenue for the self-publisher to explore. They often require a large capital outlay, but the quality of the book offsets this and the overall cost per book is less dependent on the volume ordered.

So what does that all mean? If you were to print one book through IngraSpark or KDP for $6.90, it would cost $6.90 per book, even if you ordered 2000 copies. (That is a whopping $13800)

Compare that to a printer, if you ordered 2000 copies it would cost $2.82 per book (so $5640) well under half the cost and the quality of the books would be far superior.

The other factor you should consider when using a print service is you will need to manage your own distribution. You could still list the book on Amazon, etc. but you will need to have the stock and manage all the shipping and handling. Alternatively, you could use all channels IngramSpark and KDP for global distribution and use your own website and author platform to sell the higher quality books. The options are limitless.

My favourite printer is Imago, I deal with the Australian office:

Imago Australia Pty Ltd.
www.imagogroup.com/au

But they do have offices in Brazil, China, France, Honk Kong, Malaysia, UK and the USA.

OK self-publishers, as with all the information I have provided in this book, it pays to do your own research. The process and guidelines change even for established companies like IngramSpark and KDP.

Use the links and information in this chapter as a starting point. Follow up on the platforms you want to use and work through the suggested documentation or tutorials they provide.

Part Ten
****

Shhhh... Secret Agent Stuff Happening!

28. LITERARY AGENTS

Let's talk LITERARY AGENTS! What are they and why do you need one?

> If you have an agent, you are much more likely to be taken seriously by editors. Lots of publishers don't accept submissions that aren't represented by a LITERARY AGENT!

Agents typically get 15 - 20% of your royalty for standard domestic rights. So why do they get this percentage of your money?

AGENTS KNOW THE BUSINESS

THEY KNOW WHAT EACH EDITOR OR PUBLISHER WANTS

THEY GET YOU A BETTER DEAL

THEY CAN GET YOU HIGHER ADVANCES

OPTIONED FOR FILM OR TV RIGHTS

AND EVEN GET YOUR BOOK TRANSLATED INTO OTHER LANGUAGES,

ALL WHICH INCREASES THE MONEY YOU CAN EARN!

The one IMPORTANT fact to know about agents is:

> AGENTS DON'T GET PAID UNTIL YOU DO!

So how do you go about getting an Agent? Each agent will have specific requirements and guidelines, from what they represent to how to send queries. But you will need a good QUERY LETTER!

A query letter should be only one page and contain specific information the agent needs to know in order to determine if they want to know more about you or your books. In the next section, we will look at the elements of a good query letter. And then there is a worksheet for you to practice filling out.

THE QUERY LETTER

INTRODUCTION

Start your letter with "Dear [First name] [Last name]", this applies whether you're submitting work digitally or by traditional post.
If you don't know the agent or editor name, then write to the Department head as outlined in their submissions guidelines such as "Dear Submissions", or Dear "Acquisitions Editor", if all else fails use "To whom it may concern."

> Double-check your spelling of names.
> Is it Peter or Peta? Jon or John?

Example: Dear Lucy Literary Agent.

OPENING PARAGRAPH

This is a single sentence that should contain the **REASON YOU ARE WRITING TO THEM**, the **TITLE, GENRE,** and **WORD COUNT** of your manuscript,

Example: I'm writing to seek representation for my new book, THOSE BEES STOLE MY CHEESE, a 32 page picture book for grades 2-4 of 183 words.

MAIN PARAGRAPH 1

This is where you explain what the book is about. You're not writing a blurb, just explaining what kind of book this is to someone who only has time to read 70-100 words.

Example: The book opens with bees stealing a child's cheese, which begs the question: WHY? In this fun filled, fast-paced story written in rhyme, our bees are on a mission, they need cheese, but when confronted by the child, they return to help the child understand how, as trustees of the planet they need to fix the problems we have created. Using bees as the avatars is a child friendly way of explaining how humanity's actions (pesticides, logging, and fossil fuels) are leading to major environmental impacts. One in particular 'varroa mite' is killing off the bees. They explain in bouncy verse what needs to be done to save the flowers, trees and the bees.

MAIN PARAGRAPH 2
Having explained what the book is, explain why your book is exciting and necessary. This is your elevator pitch: short, vivid, compelling! It may be as little as a dozen words. Tell them about your **HOOK** and what's different about your book.

Example: Those Bees Stole My Cheese uses humour, rhythm and rhyme to highlight a very important environmental issue—without the bees we'll have no trees, no flowers and ultimately no food.

AUTHOR PARAGRAPH – STANDARD
Most fiction writers can get away with very little here. Agents are interested in your manuscript. Keeping this short will work well for most authors.

Example: I am a 52-year-old Author / Illustrator living in Queensland, Australia with my wife and two amazingly creative kids.

AUTHOR PARAGRAPH – INTERESTING BACKGROUNDS
In some instances there is a genuinely interesting link between your background and the substance of the story, or perhaps you have won a major writing competitions or have some other successful publishing experience. you can add that in this section too.

Example: I have a Master's Degree in Environmental and Business Management and a Bachelor's Degree in Further Education and Training that supports not only the content of the story but also the STEM related activities in the lesson packs.

CLOSING REMARKS
If you have a genuine reason to mention why you approached a specific agent, add it here.

Example: I am seeking your representation following our discussion at the CYA conference in Brisbane, 2019. I have attached the complete manuscript for your review. I look forward to hearing from you.

PUT IT TOGETHER

Lucy Literary
Literary Agent _ Children's Books
Lucy Literary Agency
PO Box XYZ Warner LitWorld 4500

Dear Lucy Literary
I'm writing to seek representation for my new book, THOSE BEES STOLE MY CHEESE, a 32 page picture book for grades 2-4 of 183 words.

The book opens with bees stealing a child's cheese, which begs the question: WHY?

In this fun filled, fast-paced story written in rhyme, our bees are on a mission, they need cheese, but when confronted by the child, they return to help the child understand how, as trustees of the planet they need to fix the problems we have created. Using bees as the avatars is a child friendly way of explaining how humanity's actions (pesticides, logging, and fossil fuels) are leading to major environmental impacts. One in particular 'varroa mite' which is killing off the bees.

Those Bees Stole My Cheese uses humour, rhythm and rhyme to highlight a very important environmental issue—without the bees we'll have no trees, no flowers and ultimately no food.

I have a Master's Degree in Environmental and Business Management and a Bachelor's Degree in Further Education and Training that supports not only the content of the story but also the STEM related activities in the lesson packs.

I also have several other manuscripts available should you wish to see more of my work.

I am seeking your representation following our discussion at the CYA conference in Brisbane, 2019. I have attached the complete manuscript for your review. I look forward to hearing from you.

Matt B Lewis
1234 567 890
www.mattblewis.com

INTRODUCTION

OPENING PARAGRAPH

MAIN PARAGRAPH 1

MAIN PARAGRAPH 2

AUTHOR PARAGRAPH

CLOSING REMARKS

Now it's time to do some research on the internet and look for an agency that fits your book. Remember to follow their guidelines. I have listed a selection of agencies with Literary Agents currently looking for picture books to represent.

WRITERS HOUSE LLC
http://www.writershouse.com
CAA PUBLISHING
https://www.caa.com/
SANFORD GREENBERGER ASSOCIATES
http://www.greenburger.com
STONE SONG
https://www.stonesong.com/
SHELDON FOGELMAN AGENCY
http://www.sheldonfogelmanagency.com/
GALLT & ZACKER LITERARY AGENCY
https://www.galltzacker.com/
ANDREA BROWN LITERARY AGENCY
https://www.andreabrownlit.com/
THE GREENHOUSE LITERARY AGENCY LTD
http://greenhouseliterary.com
BOOKENDS LITERARY
www.bookendsliterary.com/
MARTIN LITERARY MANAGEMENT
adriagoetz.com
THE ETHAN ELLENBERG LITERARY AGENCY
https://www.ethanellenberg.com/
ROGERS, COLERIDGE AND WHITE LITERARY AGENCY
https://www.rcwlitagency.com/
JOYCE SWEENY
joycesweeney.com
FOLIO JR
http://www.foliojr.com/
TORI SHARP
https://noveltori.com/
BOOKENDS LITERARY AGENCY
https://bookendsliterary.com/
TRIADAUS LITERARY AGENCY
www.triadaus.com
ANDREA WALKER
https://andrea-walker.com/

PROSPECT AGENCY
https://www.prospectagency.com/
PIPPIN PROPERTIES
https://www.pippinproperties.com/
THE CHUDNEY AGENCY
http://thechudneyagency.com/
FULL CIRCLE LITERARY
https://www.fullcircleliterary.com/
WERNICK & PRATT AGENCY
https://wernickpratt.com/agents/
SOHO AGENCY
https://www.thesohoagency.co.uk/
PETERS FRASER AND DUNLOP GROUP
http://www.petersfraserdunlop.com/
CREATIVE AUTHORS
http://www.creativeauthors.co.uk/
LINDSAY LITERARY AGENCY
http://www.lindsayliteraryagency.co.uk
DAVID HIGHAM ASSOCIATES
http://www.davidhigham.co.uk/
MILES STOTT CHILDREN'S LITERARY AGENCY
http://www.milesstottagency.co.uk/
THE BLAIR PARTNERSHIP
http://www.theblairpartnership.com
CURTIS BROWN LTD.
https://www.curtisbrown.com/
SHEIL LAND ASSOCIATES
http://www.sheilland.co.uk
DYSTEL, GODERICH & BOURRET LLC
https://www.dystel.com/
ANDREA BROWN LITERARY AGENCY INC
https://www.andreabrownlit.com/
LR CHILDREN'S LITERARY
http://www.lrchildrensliterary.com/
WATSON LITTLE
http://www.watsonlittle.com

Janklow and Nesbit
http://www.janklowandnesbit.co.uk/
Holroyde Cartey Limited
http://www.holroydecartey.com/index.html
The Catchpole Agency
http://www.thecatchpoleagency.co.uk/
AM Heath and Co
https://amheath.com/
Anne Clark Literary Agency
http://www.anneclarkliteraryagency.co.uk/
Tibor Jones and Associates
http://tiborjones.com/
Rogers Coleridge and White
http://www.rcwlitagency.com/
Corvisiero Literary Agency
https://www.corvisieroagency.com/
Redhammer Management
http://www.redhammer.info/
Betsy Amster Literary Enterprises
https://amsterlit.com/
Folio Literary Agency, LLC
http://www.foliolit.com/
The Greenhouse Literary Agency
https://www.greenhouseliterary.com/
The Agency
https://theagency.co.uk/
Joanna Devereux Literary Agency
http://www.joannadevereux.com/
Raven Quill Literary Agency
https://ravenliterary.com/
Flannery Literary
https://flanneryliterary.com/
Fraser Ross Associates Literary Agency
http://www.fraserross.co.uk/
Trident Media Group
https://www.tridentmediagroup.com/

ANDREW NURNBERG ASSOCIATES
http://andrewnurnberg.com/

BARRY GOLDBLATT LITERARY LLC
https://bgliterary.com/

MBA LITERARY AND SCRIPT AGENTS
http://www.mbalit.co.uk/

EINSTEIN LITERARY MANAGEMENT
https://www.einsteinliterary.com/

NEW LEAF LITERARY & MEDIA INC
http://www.newleafliterary.com/

HSG AGENCY
http://www.hsgagency.com

MCINTOSH & OTIS INC.
http://mcintoshandotis.com/

SOPHIE HICKS AGENCY
http://www.sophiehicksagency.com/

UNITED AGENTS
http://www.unitedagents.co.uk/

JENNY BROWN ASSOCIATES
http://www.jennybrownassociates.com/

WHISPERING BUFFALO LITERARY AGENCY
http://www.whisperingbuffalo.com/

INTERSAGA LITERARY AGENCY
https://intersaga.co.uk/

BRADFORD LITERARY AGENCY
http://bradfordlit.com/

LBA BOOKS
http://www.lbabooks.com/

SANDRA DIJKSTRA LITERARY AGENCY
http://www.dijkstraagency.com/

THE VINEY SHAW AGENCY
http://www.thevineyagency.com/

CURTIS BROWN GROUP
http://www.curtisbrown.co.uk/

LAW AGENCY
http://www.lawagency.co.uk/

29. WHERE TO FROM HERE

JOIN THESE GROUPS

The Australian Society of Authors (ASA)

https://www.asauthors.org/

The Society of Children Book Writers and Illustrators (SCBWI)

https://www.scbwi.org/

The ASA Style File

https://asastylefile.com/

NETWORKING IS CRITICAL

- Go to conferences, retreats, festivals, and networking nights.
- Set up social media profiles FACEBOOK, INSTAGRAM, TWITTER and LINKEDIN.
- Create regular posts of your work.
- Be consistent: post the same frequency, characters, style, colour scheme etc. You need to be consistent.
- Create a one page website with –portfolio of work.
- LinkedIn – business platform – illustrating children's books is a business, so leverage the writing, illustrating and publishing sectors.
- Create a routine, set work times, and development times.
- Join Facebook groups like: 'KidsLit Writers and Illustrators', 'KidsLit Weekly Character Design' or Children's Writer's & Illustrator's Market'.
- Send your folio off to publishers – follow the guidelines and submit to publishers and/ or agents who publish in the genre and with a similar style to you.
- Join critique groups.

I want to say a very heartfelt **THANK YOU**. It takes a lot for people like us to put ourselves out there in the world. Writing books for kids, or even this book for you, opens us up to criticism and often an unwanted spotlight. Be proud of what you have accomplished!

Picture books are one of the most difficult genres to write for. Economy of words, combined with compelling visual narrative all in a truncated page count, adds a level of complexity few understand. I hope you enjoyed this book and found it helpful in finding your idea, creating engaging characters, building amazing worlds and has resulted in you crafting a picture book you are proud to read to your kids.

I congratulate you on working through all the chapters and exercises. It shows genuine commitment to your passion.

If you like what you learned in this book and want to learn more about the craft of writing and illustrating children's books, check out my website.

https://mattblewis.com/

If you are ready to take the next step, enrol in my online course

How To Write and Illustrate Picture Books

ONLINE COURSE

www.ingramcontent.com/pod-product-compliance
Lightning Source LLC
Chambersburg PA
CBHW020423010526
44118CB00010B/387